The New York Times

LOOKING FORWARD

Cryptocurrencies

BITCOIN, BLOCKCHAIN AND BEYOND

THE NEW YORK TIMES EDITORIAL STAFF

Published in 2019 by The New York Times® Educational Publishing
in association with The Rosen Publishing Group, Inc.
29 East 21st Street, New York, NY 10010

First Edition

The New York Times
Alex Ward: Editorial Director, Book Development
Phyllis Collazo: Photo Rights/Permissions Editor
Heidi Giovine: Administrative Manager

Rosen Publishing
Megan Kellerman: Managing Editor
Michael Hessel-Mial: Editor
Greg Tucker: Creative Director
Brian Garvey: Art Director

Cataloging-in-Publication Data
Names: New York Times Company.
Title: Cryptocurrencies: bitcoin, blockchain and beyond / edited
by the New York Times editorial staff.
Description: New York : New York Times Educational Publishing,
2019. | Series: Looking forward | Includes glossary and index.
Identifiers: ISBN 9781642821253 (library bound) | ISBN
9781642821246 (pbk.) | ISBN 9781642821260 (ebook)
Subjects: LCSH: Electronic commerce—Juvenile literature. |
Electronic funds transfers—Juvenile literature. | Money—Juvenile
literature. | Finance, Personal—Juvenile literature.
Classification: LCC HF5548.32 C798 2019 | DDC 332.1'78—dc23

Manufactured in the United States of America

On the cover: In this 2011 photo of bitbills — a physical
representation of the virtual currency Bitcoin — each was worth
$17; Nancy Palmieri for The New York Times.

Contents

CHAPTER 3

Bitcoin Bubbles and Busts: Behind the Volatility

Introduction

THE STORY OF BITCOIN and other cryptocurrencies centers around the concept of trust. If individuals and institutions can betray one another's trust, can exchanges be engineered trust-free? Hackers, following a libertarian tradition of keeping technological development free of government intervention, longed to create a secure digital currency. Beginning in the 1980s, privacy-obsessed "cipherpunks" experimented with encryption mechanisms to encode value into bits. These efforts mostly failed, but by the 2000s, they had taken a unique social character: As state surveillance became commonplace and financial institutions began to fail, the cipherpunks dedicated themselves to virtual currency with renewed focus.

These efforts fell into place with the advent of Bitcoin. On October 31, 2008, an unidentified author under the pseudonym Satoshi Nakamoto published a white paper titled "Bitcoin: A Peer-to-Peer Electronic Cash System." It represented the culmination of several decades of efforts to create a secure, private virtual currency. It included several innovations that, while complex, made the modern cryptocurrency economy possible. First, a peer-to-peer decentralized computing network would generate a public ledger called a "blockchain," where every transaction is made visible to avoid frauds or thefts. Ownership of Bitcoin would be verified by a process called "proof of work," which would entail devoting processing power to maintaining the network and generating new coins. To create and verify new coins would require solving specialized mathematical problems, taking a certain amount of computer power. To create scarcity, the number of possible coins was limited by doubling the amount of work required to generate coins after a certain period of time. The Bitcoin network would be

A monitor in the Coinbase office, one of the largest cryptocurrency exchanges, displaying the value of several virtual currencies in December 2017.

made secure and private through a system of public and private keys to keep all parties private, while conducting all exchanges in public. To summarize these features, decentralized networks of computers would generate coins that people can trade for goods and services over a secure public ledger. Bitcoin, considered "digital gold," is the most prestigious cryptocurrency, with all other cryptocurrencies following its basic architecture.

Only one question remained: Who will use them? Bitcoin was first widely adopted as a private currency for illegal activity but eventually saw mainstream adoption and investment. Today, countless businesses accept Bitcoin and other virtual currencies as payment, just like regular money. However, the primary business of cryptocurrency does not yet function like a traditional currency at all. Instead, cryptocurrency investments function somewhere between a commodity investment — like gold or silver — and an investment in an emerging technology. The enormous cryptocurrency "mines" — where powerful computers run algorithms to generate new coins — are an emblem of this tendency to treat Bitcoin and other virtual currencies like commodities. Many ask: Where is the real value of cryptocurrencies? Are they just another fad? While the active trading and speculation of cryptocurrencies fuel suspicion that they offer little real-world value, the remaining promise is in the technology itself. For some cryptocurrency advocates, the technology is a platform for a decentralized internet. While companies like Google, Amazon and Facebook command the bulk of traffic, server power and revenue from the internet of today, cryptocurrency developers see their work as building an independent internet again, with the coins themselves as a means of paying for it.

The cryptocurrency economy of the future is one of automated "smart contracts" that pay for traffic and processing power, AI-guided investment firms, "crypto utopias" in developing nations and coin values trending increasingly skyward. The cryptocurrency economy of the present, by contrast, showcases many of the tensions of the globalized world: investment bubbles, a rising China and a digital marketplace where the old rules no longer apply. A year from the time this introduction is written, cryptocurrencies will have likely changed dramatically: either continuing to inflate in value or crashing back to the nominal value of Bitcoin's humble origins. Whether virtual money has real value worthy of the tremendous financial risk is a question most investors have no answer for. Instead, the viability of the technology becomes a question of trust, an investment of hope that a "trust-free" computer protocol can be successful.

CHAPTER 1

The Search for a Private Virtual Currency

When Bitcoin was first invented and produced by hobbyists in the years between 2009 and 2013, it received relatively little coverage from The New York Times. Economist Paul Krugman, notably, penned the first such article for his New York Times blog in 2011. Other articles provide evidence of pundits and early adopters attempting for the first time to understand and explain Bitcoin: the technology for generating value, its security and its appeal.

Golden Cyberfetters

OPINION | BY PAUL KRUGMAN | SEPT. 7, 2011

OVER THE PAST few months a number of people have asked what I think of Bitcoin, an attempt to create a sort of private cybercurrency. Now Alexander Kowalski at Bloomberg News directs me to this Jim Surowiecki article on Bitcoin, which is very interesting.

My first reaction to Bitcoin was to say, what's new? We have lots of ways of making payments electronically; in fact, a lot of the conventional monetary system is already virtual, relying on digital accounting rather than green pieces of paper. But it turns out that there is a difference: Bitcoin, rather than fixing the value of the virtual currency in terms of those green pieces of paper, fixes the total quantity of cybercurrency instead, and lets its dollar value float. In effect, Bitcoin has created its own private gold standard world, in which the money supply is fixed rather than subject to increase via the printing press.

So how's it going? The dollar value of that cybercurrency has fluctuated sharply, but overall it has soared. So buying into Bitcoin has, at least so far, been a good investment.

But does that make the experiment a success? Um, no. What we want from a monetary system isn't to make people holding money rich; we want it to facilitate transactions and make the economy as a whole rich. And that's not at all what is happening in Bitcoin.

Bear in mind that dollar prices have been relatively stable over the past few years — yes, some deflation in 2008–2009, then some inflation as commodity prices rebounded, but overall consumer prices are only slightly higher than they were three years ago. What that means is that if you measure prices in Bitcoins, they have plunged; the Bitcoin economy has in effect experienced massive deflation.

And because of that, there has been an incentive to hoard the virtual currency rather than spending it. The actual value of transactions in Bitcoins has fallen rather than rising. In effect, real gross Bitcoin product has fallen sharply.

So to the extent that the experiment tells us anything about monetary regimes, it reinforces the case against anything like a new gold standard — because it shows just how vulnerable such a standard would be to money-hoarding, deflation, and depression.

Virtual Currency Gains Ground in Actual World

BY KATE MURPHY | JULY 31, 2013

DEPENDING ON WHOM you ask, bitcoins are a goofy geek invention with as much long-term value as Monopoly money — or a technology development that could transform currency the way e-mail and texting have transformed correspondence.

A type of digital cash, bitcoins were invented in 2009 and can be sent directly to anyone, anywhere in the world. You don't have to go through a financial institution, which means no fees and no one tracking your spending habits. With a current market capitalization of $1 billion, bitcoins are beginning to be more widely accepted. You can use them to pay for a pizza or make speculative bets that could end up financing your child's college education.

But bitcoins, and other digital currencies, have also come under scrutiny. Liberty Reserve, an online payment system, was shuttered in the spring by New York authorities, who said the company used its digital currency, known as LRs, to launder up to $6 billion. And law enforcement officials have voiced concerns that bitcoins could also abet illegal transactions. Bart Chilton, a commissioner on the Commodity Futures Trading Commission, suggested that bitcoins might be ripe for regulation.

Moreover, some critics say the bitcoin infrastructure is insecure, as hackable as any other computer-based system.

"The way the basic bitcoin system works is both incredibly solid and incredibly clever from a technical standpoint," said Nicholas Weaver, senior staff researcher at the International Computer Science Institute in Berkeley, which studies and advances a range of emerging technologies. "The system's security is fragile, however, and the economic model behind bitcoin is, well, crazy stupid."

Nonetheless, paying with bitcoins can be a weirdly fun way to make transactions. Here is a primer on how to do it.

Like gold, bitcoins, which are both a currency and a commodity, are in limited supply (there is a cap of 21 million total) and have to be "mined" before they are put in circulation. Anyone can mine for bitcoins by downloading software, known as the bitcoin client, which algorithmically crunches a bunch of numbers to legitimize or authenticate a sequence or "block" of past bitcoin transactions. So bitcoins are basically minted as a reward for contributing to the smooth operation of the system. Validating a block yields 25 bitcoins, which are currently worth $2,675.

The fluctuating price of bitcoins, also like gold, is a function of supply and demand, as well as psychology. "Bitcoins have value because people say they have value," said Andrew White, a former I.T. manager for the Wikimedia Foundation and now a digital currency entrepreneur in San Francisco.

Unlike fiat currencies like the United States dollar and virtual currencies like Facebook credits and the one invented by Liberty Reserve, bitcoins are not created or controlled by a central authority. But with the blistering rate of bitcoin transactions these days, you need a pricey and complex computer rig to effectively run the bitcoin client and procure some bitcoin bounty. An easier way to get bitcoins is to just find someone willing to sell them to you.

Julian Tosh, an I.T. systems administrator in Las Vegas, for example, lets friends and family buy items on his Amazon wish list and pays them back in bitcoins. "This works well as long as I need stuff," said Mr. Tosh, who also presides over a Wednesday "Bitcoin Lunch Mob" in Las Vegas, which gathers to discuss and trade bitcoins.

But maybe you don't personally know any bitcoin enthusiasts like Mr. Tosh or the Winklevoss twins, Cameron and Tyler, who own around $11 million worth and have filed papers with the Securities and Exchange Commission to form a bitcoin investment trust. If so, you might try localbitcoins.com, which lists people in your area who are willing to exchange bitcoins for cold hard cash. The market price Tuesday afternoon was $107 for a bitcoin. Be sure to check out sellers' profiles and reviews to make sure they are reputable. And, of course, it's always a good idea to meet in a public place to make the transaction.

Bitcoins can be easily transferred and stored using a digital wallet app on your Android mobile device. Popular wallet apps include BitcoinSpinner and Bitcoin Wallet. There are no iOS bitcoin wallet apps and Apple did not respond to e-mails seeking an explanation. But Blockchain has an online wallet service that you can access using any Internet-connected desktop, laptop, tablet or smartphone.

You can also get bitcoins through Mt.Gox, the largest bitcoin exchange and where the currency is traded as a commodity. But it's a cumbersome and lengthy process, requiring wire transfers and scanning identity documents. The company, which is based in Japan, also charges a 0.6 percent fee for all transactions.

Keep in mind that the United States Department of Homeland Security in May seized Mt.Gox's United States accounts, saying it misrepresented the full extent of its financial operations. The company did not respond to requests for comment but continues to function as before the seizure.

Another option is Coinbase, a bitcoin transaction platform, which recently announced a $5 million infusion of venture capital. While it's still a nascent venture (not even a year old), the service hasn't had any major hiccups yet and is relatively simple to use. You just enter your bank account and routing number, how many bitcoins you want and click "buy." You can also send bitcoins to others through your Coinbase account. Just know you'll be charged a 1 percent transaction fee.

Once you have your bitcoins, the fun part is spending them. Bitcoin.travel, BitcoinsInVegas.com, Spendbitcoins.com and Reddit have directories of businesses that accept bitcoins as payment. And Bitpremier.com lists high-priced luxury items (cars, jets, yachts, etc.) you can buy with bitcoins.

To make a purchase, all you have to do is type the receiver's key code or scan their QR code into your bitcoin wallet and you're done.

Like cash transactions, you can't cancel payment later, so be sure it's what you want before you click "send."

Brewster Kahle, a founder of the Internet Archive in San Francisco, said he routinely used bitcoins to pay for lunch at a local sushi restaurant. He's interested in the technology and appreciates the libertarian aspect of it. "Bitcoin used to be just in the land of computer geeks, but not anymore," he said.

More businesses are accepting bitcoins lately thanks to Bitpay, which supplies software for processing bitcoin payments. The merchant pays a 0.99 percent fee per transaction versus the 2 to 4 percent fees charged by credit card companies. Bitpay will also immediately convert bitcoins to dollars if the merchant desires.

"Bitcoin users are pretty enthusiastic, so you get instant loyal customers," said Adam Penn, owner of Veggie Galaxy, a restaurant in Cambridge, Mass., which began accepting bitcoins through Bitpay in May. "So far, it's been a no-risk revenue generator."

Also last month, Bitpay announced a partnership with the mobile gift card app Gyft, which will allow people to use bitcoins to purchase

A type of digital cash, Bitcoins were invented in 2009 and can be sent directly to anyone, anywhere in the world.

gift cards from hundreds of retailers including Brookstone, Lowe's, Gap, Sephora, GameStop, American Eagle, Nike, Marriott, Burger King and Fandango.

"It's a huge development," said Mr. Tosh in Las Vegas, who predicts Gyft's embrace of bitcoins will lead to widespread use of the alternative currency. "Pandora's box has been smashed."

Or maybe not. The legal trouble at Mt.Gox sent a shiver through the market as did S.E.C. charges last week that the founder and operator of the lesser-known Bitcoin Savings and Trust in McKinney, Tex., was running a bitcoin Ponzi scheme.

Still, bitcoin advocates point out that, despite some bad actors, the actual system has not had a major security breach. Nevertheless, even the most ardent bitcoin boosters urge caution. Bitcoins have appreciated more than 700 percent since this time last year — an increase some have compared to a bubble bound to burst.

"It's supervolatile, so I'd tell people to go slow," said Peter Vessenes, chairman and executive director of the Bitcoin Foundation, a nonprofit organization that promotes the currency. "Never hold more bitcoins than you're prepared to lose."

A Bitcoin Puzzle: Heads, It's Excitement. Tails, It's Anxiety.

BY JEFF SOMMER | NOV. 23, 2013

BITCOIN ISN'T READY for popular consumption, and it may never be.

It doesn't fit into a neat product category. Often called a virtual currency, it's not legal tender anywhere on the planet. It's not an income-generating asset class suitable for most investors. Its value, in dollars, fluctuates wildly from one minute to the next. And while it can be a cheap way of transferring money, there are too many glitches in its emerging network for Bitcoin to be entirely reliable.

Even its advocates have been raising red flags. As Patrick Murck, general counsel for the Bitcoin Foundation, a nonprofit devoted to "fostering the bitcoin ecosystem," acknowledged in a Senate hearing last week, "It's very much still an experimental currency and it should be considered a high-risk environment for consumers and investors at the moment."

Yet Bitcoin has been receiving plenty of attention, and not just because well-publicized speculators have been making money on it.

High-risk experiment though it may be, Bitcoin embodies an elegant and disruptive technology. It uses file-sharing, the peer-to-peer computer innovation that spawned early music services like Napster, Kazaa and LimeWire. In their early days, they sometimes walked on the wild side, but their experiences led to a wholesale digital transformation of the music business.

Bitcoin gives file-sharing a brilliant twist. In essence, it has created "a decentralized virtual currency that uses a peer-to-peer consensus system to confirm and verify transactions," two researchers at the Federal Reserve Bank of St. Louis concluded in a recent study. And François R. Velde, a senior economist at the Federal Reserve Bank of Chicago, made this assessment in a new report on Bitcoin: "It represents a remarkable conceptual and technical achievement, which may well be used by existing financial institutions (which could issue their own bitcoins) or even by governments themselves."

Bitcoin's advantages as a low-cost means of transferring money have intrigued a number of corporate clients of the law firm Proskauer, though none of them are using it, said Jeffrey D. Neuberger, co-chairman of the firm's technology, media and communications group. "It's an early-stage technology," he said. "But it could be revolutionary." In short, in a world that some people consider almost as important as music — the precincts of money and finance — Bitcoin, or a successor technology that shares its DNA, is given a good chance of influencing the future.

That's what made last week's hearing of the Senate Homeland Security and Governmental Affairs Committee so intriguing. It assessed the "potential risks, threats and promises of virtual currencies," with Bitcoin foremost among them. So what is Bitcoin today? Senator Thomas R. Carper, Democrat of Delaware and chairman of the committee, acknowledged that he wasn't sure how to make sense of it: "Virtual currencies, perhaps most notably Bitcoin, have captured the imagination of some, struck fear among others and confused the heck out of the rest of us, including me."

The Senate committee's attempt to get a grip on the digital currency was, in a way, the first step in what will surely be a continuing tension. On one side are those seeking ease and anonymity in transactions; on the other is the government.

Speculators and money launderers have already found much to like about the relatively anonymous digital currency, and that has forced the government to play catch-up. Bitcoin allowed the website Silk Road, which the government shut down in October, to become "the largest illegal drug and contraband marketplace on the Internet," according to Jennifer Shasky Calvery, the director of the Treasury's Financial Crimes Enforcement Network. While it was in business, customers "were required to pay in bitcoins to enable both the operator of Silk Road and its sellers to evade detection and launder hundreds of millions of dollars," she said.

The virtual currency isn't impervious to determined government snooping, however. "We are innovating as criminals are innovating," said Mythili Raman, an acting assistant attorney general, at the hearing. Individual Bitcoin transactions are encoded, but large numbers of them may be compared statistically with other databases available to the government, and patterns will emerge, several experts said.

While Bitcoin users need a secret, numerical key to unlock their accounts, the anonymity of the system is vulnerable when the virtual currency is exchanged into dollars. Federal and state authorities are requiring firms that exchange Bitcoin into currency, or use it to transfer funds, to comply with existing regulations. But when the movement from Bitcoin to hard currency takes place in a country where American authorities don't have access, "there may be opportunities for money-laundering," said Mr. Neuberger at Proskauer.

The S.E.C., for its part, has been warning investors of the danger of "potential investment scams" involving Bitcoin and other virtual currencies. In one case, it has charged Trendon T. Shavers, a Texas man, with running a Bitcoin-based Ponzi scheme with the promise of vast riches.

"Con men read the headlines like everyone else," said Lori Schock, director of the S.E.C.'s Office of Investor Education and Advocacy. "Bitcoins sound sexy and new, but at the end of the day, if they're making claims about limitless wealth from unregistered investments it comes down to an old-fashioned Ponzi scheme."

The agency is also studying a legitimate Bitcoin proposal by Cameron and Tyler Winklevoss, the technology investors best known for their involvement with Facebook, to open an exchange-traded fund, or E.T.F., that tracks the Bitcoin market. If the E.T.F. is ever approved, a fund based on a volatile virtual currency is hardly likely to be a safe, core holding for buy-and-hold investors.

In the meantime, the virtual currency's soaring value has inspired tales like this one: Kristoffer Koch, 29, of Oslo, told the BBC last month that he bought $22 worth of the currency while doing technical research on it four years ago. He promptly forgot about it. When he unlocked his long dormant account recently, it was worth $850,000.

Even with all of its problems, the eventual creation of a reliable, decentralized, peer-shared, computer-based currency remains the holy grail in some circles. Back in 1999, Milton Friedman, the Nobel laureate who remains the guiding light of many libertarians, predicted its eventual arrival. He saw the Internet as a congenial environment for innovators. Markets would flourish in cyberspace, freeing people from what he considered the stifling grasp of a paternalistic and inefficient government. But one ingredient was missing, he said. He called it "a reliable e-cash."

What was required, he said, was e-cash that enabled you to "transfer funds from A to B, without A knowing B or B knowing A — the way in which I can take a $20 bill and hand it over to you and there's no record of where it came from. And you may get that without knowing who I am."

Unfortunately, that would create new problems, he said, because such a currency would have "a negative side."

"The gangsters," he said, "the people who are engaging in illegal transactions, will also have an easier way to carry on their business."

That tension is part of progress, he said. It may be where we find ourselves now.

Why Bitcoin Matters

BY MARC ANDREESSEN | JAN. 21, 2014

Editor's note: Marc Andreessen's venture capital firm, Andreessen Horowitz, has invested just under $50 million in Bitcoin-related start-ups. The firm is actively searching for more Bitcoin-based investment opportunities. He does not personally own more than a de minimis amount of Bitcoin.

A MYSTERIOUS NEW technology emerges, seemingly out of nowhere, but actually the result of two decades of intense research and development by nearly anonymous researchers.

Political idealists project visions of liberation and revolution onto it; establishment elites heap contempt and scorn on it.

On the other hand, technologists — nerds — are transfixed by it. They see within it enormous potential and spend their nights and weekends tinkering with it.

Eventually mainstream products, companies and industries emerge to commercialize it; its effects become profound; and later, many people wonder why its powerful promise wasn't more obvious from the start.

What technology am I talking about? Personal computers in 1975, the Internet in 1993, and — I believe — Bitcoin in 2014.

One can hardly accuse Bitcoin of being an uncovered topic, yet the gulf between what the press and many regular people believe Bitcoin is, and what a growing critical mass of technologists believe Bitcoin is, remains enormous. In this post, I will explain why Bitcoin has so many Silicon Valley programmers and entrepreneurs all lathered up, and what I think Bitcoin's future potential is.

First, Bitcoin at its most fundamental level is a breakthrough in computer science — one that builds on 20 years of research into cryptographic currency, and 40 years of research in cryptography, by thousands of researchers around the world.

Bitcoin is the first practical solution to a longstanding problem in computer science called the Byzantine Generals Problem. To quote from the original paper defining the B.G.P.: "[Imagine] a group of generals of the Byzantine army camped with their troops around an enemy city. Communicating only by messenger, the generals must agree upon a common battle plan. However, one or more of them may be traitors who will try to confuse the others. The problem is to find an algorithm to ensure that the loyal generals will reach agreement."

More generally, the B.G.P. poses the question of how to establish trust between otherwise unrelated parties over an untrusted network like the Internet.

The practical consequence of solving this problem is that Bitcoin gives us, for the first time, a way for one Internet user to transfer a unique piece of digital property to another Internet user, such that the transfer is guaranteed to be safe and secure, everyone knows that the transfer has taken place, and nobody can challenge the legitimacy of the transfer. The consequences of this breakthrough are hard to overstate.

What kinds of digital property might be transferred in this way? Think about digital signatures, digital contracts, digital keys (to physical locks, or to online lockers), digital ownership of physical assets such as cars and houses, digital stocks and bonds ... and digital money.

All these are exchanged through a distributed network of trust that does not require or rely upon a central intermediary like a bank or broker. And all in a way where only the owner of an asset can send it, only the intended recipient can receive it, the asset can only exist in one place at a time, and everyone can validate transactions and ownership of all assets anytime they want.

How does this work?

Bitcoin is an Internet-wide distributed ledger. You buy into the ledger by purchasing one of a fixed number of slots, either with cash or by selling a product and service for Bitcoin. You sell out of the ledger by trading your Bitcoin to someone else who wants to buy into the ledger. Anyone in the world can buy into or sell out of the ledger any time they want — with no approval needed, and with no or very low fees. The Bitcoin "coins" themselves are simply slots in the ledger, analogous in some ways to seats on a stock exchange, except much more broadly applicable to real world transactions.

The Bitcoin ledger is a new kind of payment system. Anyone in the world can pay anyone else in the world any amount of value of Bitcoin by simply transferring ownership of the corresponding slot in the ledger. Put value in, transfer it, the recipient gets value out, no authorization required, and in many cases, no fees.

That last part is enormously important. Bitcoin is the first Internet-wide payment system where transactions either happen with no fees or very low fees (down to fractions of pennies). Existing payment systems charge fees of about 2 to 3 percent — and that's in the developed world. In lots of other places, there either are no modern payment systems or the rates are significantly higher. We'll come back to that.

Bitcoin is a digital bearer instrument. It is a way to exchange money or assets between parties with no pre-existing trust: A string of numbers is sent over email or text message in the simplest case. The sender doesn't need to know or trust the receiver or vice versa. Related, there are no chargebacks — this is the part that is literally like cash — if you have the money or the asset, you can pay with it; if you don't, you can't. This is brand new. This has never existed in digital form before.

Bitcoin is a digital currency, whose value is based directly on two things: use of the payment system today — volume and velocity of payments running through the ledger — and speculation on future use of the payment system. This is one part that is confusing people. It's not as much that the Bitcoin currency has some arbitrary value and then people are trading with it; it's more that people can trade with Bitcoin (anywhere, everywhere, with no fraud and no or very low fees) and as a result it has value.

It is perhaps true right at this moment that the value of Bitcoin currency is based more on speculation than actual payment volume, but it is equally true that that speculation is establishing a sufficiently high price for the currency that payments have become practically possible.

The Bitcoin currency had to be worth something before it could bear any amount of real-world payment volume. This is the classic "chicken and egg" problem with new technology: new technology is not worth much until it's worth a lot. And so the fact that Bitcoin has risen in value in part because of speculation is making the reality of its usefulness arrive much faster than it would have otherwise.

Critics of Bitcoin point to limited usage by ordinary consumers and merchants, but that same criticism was leveled against PCs and the Internet at the same stage. Every day, more and more consumers and merchants are buying, using and selling Bitcoin, all around the world. The overall numbers are still small, but they are growing quickly. And ease of use for all participants is rapidly increasing as Bitcoin tools and technologies are improved. Remember, it used to be technically challenging to even get on the Internet. Now it's not.

The criticism that merchants will not accept Bitcoin because of its volatility is also incorrect. Bitcoin can be used entirely as a payment system; merchants do not need to hold any Bitcoin currency or be exposed to Bitcoin volatility at any time. Any consumer or merchant can trade in and out of Bitcoin and other currencies any time they want.

Why would any merchant — online or in the real world — want to accept Bitcoin as payment, given the currently small number of consumers who want to pay with it? My partner Chris Dixon recently gave this example:

"Let's say you sell electronics online. Profit margins in those businesses are usually under 5 percent, which means conventional 2.5 percent payment fees consume half the margin. That's money that could be reinvested in the business, passed back to consumers or taxed by the government. Of all of those choices, handing 2.5 percent to banks to move bits around the Internet is the worst possible choice. Another challenge merchants have with payments is accepting international payments. If you are wondering why your favorite product or service isn't available in your country, the answer is often payments."

In addition, merchants are highly attracted to Bitcoin because it eliminates the risk of credit card fraud. This is the form of fraud that motivates so many criminals to put so much work into stealing personal customer information and credit card numbers.

Since Bitcoin is a digital bearer instrument, the receiver of a payment does not get any information from the sender that can be used to steal money from the sender in the future, either by that merchant or by a criminal who steals that information from the merchant.

Credit card fraud is such a big deal for merchants, credit card processors and banks that online fraud detection systems are hair-trigger wired to stop transactions that look even slightly suspicious, whether or not they are actually fraudulent. As a result, many online merchants are forced to turn away 5 to 10 percent of incoming orders that they could take without fear if the customers were paying with Bitcoin, where such fraud would not be possible. Since these are orders that were coming in already, they are inherently the highest margin orders a merchant can get, and so being able to take them will drastically increase many merchants' profit margins.

Bitcoin's antifraud properties even extend into the physical world of retail stores and shoppers.

For example, with Bitcoin, the huge hack that recently stole 70 million consumers' credit card information from the Target department store chain would not have been possible. Here's how that would work:

You fill your cart and go to the checkout station like you do now. But instead of handing over your credit card to pay, you pull out your smartphone and take a snapshot of a QR code displayed by the cash register. The QR code contains all the information required for you to send Bitcoin to Target, including the amount. You click "Confirm" on your phone and the transaction is done (including converting dollars from your account into Bitcoin, if you did not own any Bitcoin).

Target is happy because it has the money in the form of Bitcoin, which it can immediately turn into dollars if it wants, and it paid no or very low payment processing fees; you are happy because there is no way for hackers to steal any of your personal information; and organized crime is unhappy. (Well, maybe criminals are still happy: They can try to steal money directly from poorly-secured merchant computer systems. But even if they succeed, consumers bear no risk of loss, fraud or identity theft.)

Finally, I'd like to address the claim made by some critics that Bitcoin is a haven for bad behavior, for criminals and terrorists to transfer money anonymously with impunity. This is a myth, fostered mostly by sensationalistic press coverage and an incomplete understanding of the technology. Much like email, which is quite traceable, Bitcoin is pseudonymous, not anonymous. Further, every transaction in the Bitcoin network is tracked and logged forever in the Bitcoin blockchain, or permanent record, available for all to see. As a result, Bitcoin is considerably easier for law enforcement to trace than cash, gold or diamonds.

What's the future of Bitcoin?

Bitcoin is a classic network effect, a positive feedback loop. The more people who use Bitcoin, the more valuable Bitcoin is for everyone who uses it, and the higher the incentive for the next user to start using the technology. Bitcoin shares this network effect property with the telephone system, the web, and popular Internet services like eBay and Facebook.

In fact, Bitcoin is a four-sided network effect. There are four constituencies that participate in expanding the value of Bitcoin as a consequence of their own self-interested participation. Those constituencies are (1) consumers who pay with Bitcoin, (2) merchants who accept Bitcoin, (3) "miners" who run the computers that process and validate all the transactions and enable the distributed trust network to exist, and (4) developers and entrepreneurs who are building new products and services with and on top of Bitcoin.

All four sides of the network effect are playing a valuable part in expanding the value of the overall system, but the fourth is particularly important.

All over Silicon Valley and around the world, many thousands of programmers are using Bitcoin as a building block for a kaleidoscope of new product and service ideas that were not possible before. And at our venture capital firm, Andreessen Horowitz, we are seeing a rapidly increasing number of outstanding entrepreneurs — not a few with highly respected track records in the financial industry — building companies on top of Bitcoin.

For this reason alone, new challengers to Bitcoin face a hard uphill battle. If something is to displace Bitcoin now, it will have to have sizable improvements and it will have to happen quickly. Otherwise, this network effect will carry Bitcoin to dominance.

One immediately obvious and enormous area for Bitcoin-based innovation is international remittance. Every day, hundreds of millions of low-income people go to work in hard jobs in foreign countries to make money to send back to their families in their home countries — over $400 billion in total annually, according to the World Bank. Every day, banks and payment companies extract mind-boggling fees, up to 10 percent and sometimes even higher, to send this money.

Switching to Bitcoin, which charges no or very low fees, for these remittance payments will therefore raise the quality of life of migrant workers and their families significantly. In fact, it is hard to think of any one thing that would have a faster and more positive effect on so many people in the world's poorest countries.

Moreover, Bitcoin generally can be a powerful force to bring a much larger number of people around the world into the modern economic system. Only about 20 countries around the world have what we would consider to be fully modern banking and payment systems; the other roughly 175 have a long way to go. As a result, many people in many countries are excluded from products and services that we in the West take for granted. Even Netflix, a completely virtual service, is only available in about 40 countries. Bitcoin, as a global payment system anyone can use from anywhere at any time, can be a powerful catalyst to extend the benefits of the modern economic system to virtually everyone on the planet.

And even here in the United States, a long-recognized problem is the extremely high fees that the "unbanked" — people without conventional bank accounts — pay for even basic financial services. Bitcoin can be used to go straight at that problem, by making it easy to offer extremely low-fee services to people outside of the traditional financial system.

A third fascinating use case for Bitcoin is micropayments, or ultra-small payments. Micropayments have never been feasible, despite 20 years of attempts, because it is not cost effective to run small payments (think $1 and below, down to pennies or fractions of a penny) through the existing credit/debit and banking systems. The fee structure of those systems makes that nonviable.

All of a sudden, with Bitcoin, that's trivially easy. Bitcoins have the nifty property of infinite divisibility: currently down to eight decimal places after the dot, but more in the future. So you can specify an arbitrarily small amount of money, like a thousandth of a penny, and send it to anyone in the world for free or near-free.

Think about content monetization, for example. One reason media businesses such as newspapers struggle to charge for content is because they need to charge either all (pay the entire subscription fee for all the content) or nothing (which then results in all those terrible banner ads everywhere on the web). All of a sudden, with Bitcoin, there is an economically viable way to charge arbitrarily small amounts of money per article, or per section, or per hour, or per video play, or per archive access, or per news alert.

Another potential use of Bitcoin micropayments is to fight spam. Future email systems and social networks could refuse to accept incoming messages unless they were accompanied with tiny amounts of Bitcoin — tiny enough to not matter to the sender, but large enough to deter spammers, who today can send uncounted billions of spam messages for free with impunity.

Finally, a fourth interesting use case is public payments. This idea first came to my attention in a news article a few months ago. A random spectator at a televised sports event held up a placard with a QR code and the text "Send me Bitcoin!" He received $25,000 in Bitcoin in the first 24 hours, all from people he had never met. This was the first time in history that you could see someone holding up a sign, in person or on TV or in a photo, and then send them money with two clicks on your smartphone: take the photo of the QR code on the sign, and click to send the money.

Think about the implications for protest movements. Today protesters want to get on TV so people learn about their cause. Tomorrow they'll want to get on TV because that's how they'll raise money, by literally holding up signs that let people anywhere in the world who sympathize with them send them money on the spot. Bitcoin is a financial technology dream come true for even the most hardened anticapitalist political organizer.

The coming years will be a period of great drama and excitement revolving around this new technology.

For example, some prominent economists are deeply skeptical of Bitcoin, even though Ben S. Bernanke, formerly Federal Reserve chairman, recently wrote that digital currencies like Bitcoin "may hold long-term promise, particularly if they promote a faster, more secure and more efficient payment system." And in 1999, the legendary economist Milton Friedman said: "One thing that's missing but will soon be developed is a reliable e-cash, a method whereby on the Internet you can transfer funds from A to B without A knowing B or B knowing A — the way I can take a $20 bill and hand it over to you, and you may get that without knowing who I am."

Economists who attack Bitcoin today might be correct, but I'm with Ben and Milton.

Further, there is no shortage of regulatory topics and issues that will have to be addressed, since almost no country's regulatory framework for banking and payments anticipated a technology like Bitcoin.

But I hope that I have given you a sense of the enormous promise of Bitcoin. Far from a mere libertarian fairy tale or a simple Silicon

Valley exercise in hype, Bitcoin offers a sweeping vista of opportunity to reimagine how the financial system can and should work in the Internet era, and a catalyst to reshape that system in ways that are more powerful for individuals and businesses alike.

The Bitcoin Ideology

BY ALAN FEUER | DEC. 14, 2013

IF YOU'VE ONLY recently tuned in to the seemingly endless conversation about Bitcoin, you could be forgiven for thinking that the digital currency is little more than the latest Wall Street fetish or a juiced-up version of PayPal. After all, so many headlines in the last few weeks have focused on its market price and the cool stuff you can get with it: Bitcoin breaks $1,000! Bitcoin plunges by a half! Bitcoin has a banner Black Friday! Use Bitcoin to buy a ride on Richard Branson's starship!

But all the talk about Bitcoin's value (or lack thereof) obscures the fact that it was never really meant as an investment nor primarily as a way to purchase sex toys or alpaca socks — let alone a brand-new Lamborghini. One could argue that Bitcoin isn't chiefly a commercial venture at all, a funny thing to say about a kind of online cash. To its creators and numerous disciples, Bitcoin is — and always has been — a mostly ideological undertaking, more philosophy than finance.

"The ideas behind it — that's what attracted me," said Elizabeth Ploshay, a regular writer for Bitcoin magazine, which describes its mission as being "the most accurate and up-to-date source of information, news and commentary about Bitcoin." And if the magazine has a mission, so, too, does the subject that it covers. As Ms. Ploshay explained it, Bitcoin isn't merely money; it's "a movement" — a crusade in the costume of a currency. Depending on whom you talk to, the goal is to unleash repressed economies, to take down global banking or to wage a war against the Federal Reserve.

For those with an uncertain understanding of its history, Bitcoin entered the world on Jan. 3, 2009, when a shadowy hacker — or team of hackers — working under the name Satoshi Nakamoto released an ingenious string of computer code that established a system permitting people to transfer money to one another online, directly, anonymously and outside government control, in much the way that Napster once allowed the unrestrained transfer of music files. In a 500-word essay that accompanied the code, Nakamoto suggested that the motive for creating Bitcoin was anger at the financial crisis: "The root problem with conventional currencies is all the trust that's required to make it work. The central bank must be trusted not to debase the currency, but the history of fiat currencies is full of breaches of that trust."

It was fundamentally a political document and, as such, it attracted followers among libertarian and anarchist groups who saw in Bitcoin a means of removing the money supply from the grasping hands of government. In blog posts and at Bitcoin conferences around the globe, these evangelists began to spread its gospel. It is only in the last few months, as Bitcoin has attracted the attention of political parties, regulators and speculative investors that the narrative of Bitcoin as a tool for change has been drowned out by a simpler story line: that of Bitcoin as a kind of crypto-credit card — or, even more, as a digitized casino game.

"Price is the least interesting thing about Bitcoin," said Roger Ver, an early investor who is often called, in a typical movement phrase, the Bitcoin Jesus. "At first, almost everyone who got involved did so for philosophical reasons. We saw Bitcoin as a great idea, as a way to separate money from the state."

While the Bitcoin hype has inspired Ron Paulian dreams of evading inflation and undermining the Federal Reserve, the currency has also gained cachet among less conspicuously conservative adherents, like the founders of BitPesa, a start-up firm in Nairobi, Kenya, that plans to help Africans abroad send money to their families at home. According to the World Bank, $1.3 billion in remittances is sent each year to Kenya, a process that costs about $110 million in fees. By using Bitcoin's peer-to-peer technology to avoid banks and wire-transfer companies like Western Union, BitPesa hopes to reduce these fees by two-thirds, saving ordinary Africans $74 million annually.

You know you're talking to a true Bitcoin believer if you hear the word "disruption." But that's how Bitcoin is seen within the broader movement: as an unruly tool with potentially transformative effects on entrenched businesses like retail payment and asset management.

"Right now in the United States, Bitcoin is mainly considered a get-rich-quick scheme with a little financial privacy thrown in," said Jon Matonis, the executive director of the Bitcoin Foundation, the self-proclaimed center of the decentralized crusade. "But its larger implications down the road are major disruptions to certain legacy industries."

Mr. Matonis added that the ideology of Bitcoin was wide enough to accommodate people on all points on the spectrum — "from libertarian capitalists to socialists." It not only has a following among the anti-central bank crowd, he said; it has also proved attractive to communitarians like the residents of the Kreuzberg neighborhood in Berlin, which now boasts the highest density of businesses accepting Bitcoin in the world.

There are even those who see Bitcoin as the ultimate alternative to the global banking system. Ryan Singer, a co-founder of the Bitcoin exchange Tradehill, based in San Francisco, compared the currency to email, conjecturing that it would gradually supplant traditional banking, just as digital messaging displaced handwritten letters. "When kids wake up to the fact that they don't need their parents' help to create a Bitcoin wallet," Mr. Singer said, "when they can use bitcoins for free international transactions, at any hour, in every major city on the planet, then you'll know that something has changed."

Perhaps the best proof of Bitcoin's ideological underpinnings is that a schism has emerged in recent weeks between moderate elements in the movement who sense the necessity of cooperating with officialdom, and a more uncompromising faction that wants to keep Bitcoin free from any government regulation. The hard-line bloc is exemplified by the crypto-anarchist developers of a Bitcoin product called Dark Wallet, which is scheduled to be introduced next year and will include extra protections to ensure that Bitcoin transactions remain secure, anonymous and difficult to trace.

"We see this as part of the total sublation of the state," said Cody Wilson, Dark Wallet's director, who gained fame earlier this year when he published online the blueprints to a pistol that could be manufactured with a 3-D printer. "I know I sound like some kind of weird Jehovah's Witness, but we've only just begun. We admit that we are ideologues."

Decoding the Enigma of Satoshi Nakamoto and the Birth of Bitcoin

BY NATHANIEL POPPER | MAY 15, 2015

IT IS ONE of the great mysteries of the digital age.

The hunt for Satoshi Nakamoto, the elusive creator of Bitcoin, has captivated even those who think the virtual currency is some sort of online Ponzi scheme. A legend has emerged from a jumble of facts: Someone using the name Satoshi Nakamoto released the software for Bitcoin in early 2009 and communicated with the nascent currency's users via email — but never by phone or in person. Then, in 2011, just as the technology began to attract wider attention, the emails stopped. Suddenly, Satoshi was gone, but the stories grew larger.

Over the last year, as I worked on a book about the history of Bitcoin, it was hard to avoid being drawn in by the almost mystical riddle of Satoshi Nakamoto's identity. Just as I began my research, Newsweek made a splash with a cover article in March 2014 claiming that Satoshi was an unemployed engineer in his 60s who lived in suburban Los Angeles. Within a day of publication, however, most people knowledgeable about Bitcoin had concluded that the magazine had the wrong man.

Many in the Bitcoin community told me that, in deference to the Bitcoin creator's clear desire for privacy, they didn't want to see the wizard unmasked. But even among those who said this, few could resist debating the clues the founder left behind. As I had these conversations with the programmers and entrepreneurs who are most deeply involved in Bitcoin, I encountered a quiet but widely held belief that much of the most convincing evidence pointed to a reclusive American man of Hungarian descent named Nick Szabo.

Mr. Szabo is nearly as much of a mystery as Satoshi. But in the course of my reporting I kept turning up new hints that drew me further into the chase, and I even stumbled into a rare encounter with Mr. Szabo at a private gathering of top Bitcoin programmers and entrepreneurs.

At that event, Mr. Szabo denied that he was Satoshi, as he has consistently in electronic communications, including in an email on Wednesday. But he acknowledged that his history left little question that he was among a small group of people who, over decades, working sometimes cooperatively and sometimes in competition, laid the foundation for Bitcoin and created many parts that later went into the virtual currency. Mr. Szabo's most notable contribution was a Bitcoin predecessor known as bit gold that achieved many of the same goals using similar tools of advanced math and cryptography.

It may be impossible to prove Satoshi's identity until the person or people behind Bitcoin's curtain decide to come forward and prove ownership of Satoshi's old electronic accounts. At this point, the creator's identity is no longer important to Bitcoin's future. Since Satoshi stopped contributing to the project in 2011, most of the open-source code has been rewritten by a group of programmers whose identities are known.

But Mr. Szabo's story provides insight into often misunderstood elements of Bitcoin's creation. The software was not a bolt out of the blue, as is sometimes assumed, but was instead built on the ideas of multiple people over several decades.

This history is more than just a matter of curiosity. The software has come to be viewed in academic and financial circles as a significant computer science breakthrough that may reshape the way money looks and moves. Recently, banks like Goldman Sachs have taken the first steps toward embracing the technology.

Mr. Szabo himself has continued to be quietly involved in the work. In the beginning of 2014, Mr. Szabo joined Vaurum, a Bitcoin start-up based in Palo Alto, Calif., that was operating in stealth mode and that aimed to build a better Bitcoin exchange. After his arrival, Mr. Szabo helped reorient the company to take advantage of the Bitcoin software's capability for so-called smart contracts, which enable self-executing financial transactions, according to people briefed on the company's operations who spoke on condition of anonymity.

After Mr. Szabo led the company in a new direction, it was renamed Mirror, and it recently raised $12.5 million from several prominent venture capitalists, these people said. The company declined to comment for this article.

Mr. Szabo's role at Vaurum has been kept a secret because of his desire for privacy, and he left in late 2014 after becoming nervous about public exposure, according to the people briefed on the company's operations. While he was still there, though, the array of arcane skills and knowledge at his command led several colleagues to conclude that Mr. Szabo was most likely involved in the creation of Bitcoin, even if he didn't do it all himself.

I met Mr. Szabo, a large bearded man, in March 2014 at a Bitcoin event at the Lake Tahoe vacation home of Dan Morehead, a former Goldman Sachs executive who now runs a Bitcoin-focused investment firm, Pantera Capital. Mr. Szabo worked for Vaurum at the time. Mr. Morehead and other hedge fund executives in attendance dressed in expensive loafers and slim-cut jeans; Mr. Szabo, his bald pate encircled by a ring of salt-and-pepper hair, wore beat-up black sneakers and an untucked striped shirt.

While he kept to himself, I managed to corner him in the kitchen during the cocktail hour. He was notably reserved and deflected questions about where he lived and had worked, but he bristled when I cited what was being said about him on the Internet — including that he was a law professor at George Washington University — and the notion that he had created Bitcoin.

"Well, I will say this, in the hope of setting the record straight," he said acidly. "I'm not Satoshi, and I'm not a college professor. In fact, I never was a college professor."

The conversation grew less heated when I asked about the origin of the many complicated pieces of code and cryptography that went into the Bitcoin software, and about the small number of people who would have had the expertise to put them together. Mr. Szabo mentioned bit gold, saying it harnessed many of the same obscure concepts, like secure property titles and digital time stamps, that made Bitcoin possible.

"There are a whole bunch of parallels," he told me. "I mean, the reason people tag me is because you can go through secure property titles and bit gold — there are so many parallels between that and Bitcoin that you can't find anywhere else."

When I asked if he believed that Satoshi had been familiar with his work, Mr. Szabo said he understood why there was so much speculation about his own role: "All I'm saying is, there are all these parallels, and it looks funny to me, and looks funny to a lot of other people."

Dinner began, interrupting the conversation, and I never got another chance to talk to Mr. Szabo.

When I emailed him on Wednesday, he repeated his denial: "As I've stated many times before, all this speculation is flattering, but wrong — I am not Satoshi."

Many concepts central to Bitcoin were developed in an online community known as the Cypherpunks, a loosely organized group of digital privacy activists. As part of their mission, they set out to create digital money that would be as anonymous as physical cash. Mr. Szabo was a member, and in 1993, he wrote a message to fellow Cypherpunks describing the diverse motivations of attendees at a group meeting that had just taken place. Some people, he wrote, "are libertarians who want government out of our lives, others are liberals fighting the N.S.A., others find it great fun to ding people in power with cool hacks."

Mr. Szabo had a libertarian mind-set. He was drawn to those ideas partly, he told me, because of his father, who fought the communists in Hungary in the 1950s before coming to the United States, where Mr. Szabo was born 51 years ago. Reared in Washington State, Mr. Szabo studied computer science at the University of Washington.

Several experiments in digital cash circulated on the Cypherpunk lists in the 1990s. Adam Back, a British researcher, created one called hashcash that later became a central component of Bitcoin. Another, called b money, was designed by an intensely private computer engineer named Wei Dai.

When these experiments failed to take off, many Cypherpunks lost interest. But not Mr. Szabo. He worked for six months as a consultant for a company called DigiCash, he has written on his blog. In 1998, he sent the outline for his own version of digital money, which he called bit gold, to a small group that was still pursuing the project, including Mr. Dai and Hal Finney, a programmer based in Santa Barbara, Calif., who tried to create a working version of bit gold.

The concept behind bit gold was very similar to Bitcoin: It included a digital token that was scarce, like gold, and could be sent electronically without needing to pass through a central authority like a bank.

This history points to the important role that Mr. Szabo and several others played in developing the building blocks that went into Bitcoin. When Satoshi Nakamoto's paper describing Bitcoin appeared in the fall of 2008, it cited Mr. Back's hashcash. The first people Satoshi emailed privately were Mr. Back and Mr. Dai, both men have said. And Mr. Finney, who recently died, helped Satoshi improve the Bitcoin software in the fall of 2008, before it was publicly released, according to emails shared with me by Mr. Finney and his family.

It is, though, Mr. Szabo's activity in 2008, as Bitcoin emerged into the world, that has generated much of the suspicion about his role in the project. That spring, before anyone had ever heard of Satoshi Nakamoto or Bitcoin, Mr. Szabo revived his bit gold idea on his personal blog, and in an online conversation about creating a live version of the virtual currency, he asked his readers: "Anybody want to help me code one up?"

After Bitcoin appeared, Mr. Szabo reposted the item on his blog in a way that changed the date at the top and made it appear as though it was written after Bitcoin's release, archived versions of the website show.

Mr. Szabo's writing about bit gold from that time contains many striking parallels with Satoshi's description of Bitcoin, including similar phrasings and even common writing mannerisms. In 2014, researchers at Aston University, in England, compared the writing of several people who have been suspected to be Satoshi and found that none matched up nearly as well as Mr. Szabo's. The similarity was "uncanny," said Jack Grieve, the lecturer who led the effort.

When I went back and read Mr. Szabo's online writings, it was obvious that in the year before Satoshi appeared on the scene and released Bitcoin, Mr. Szabo was again thinking seriously about digital money.

He wrote frequently, over several months, about the concepts involved in digital money, including those smart contracts, a concept so specialized that Mr. Szabo is often given credit for inventing the term. Smart contracts later showed up as an essential piece of the Bitcoin software.

Mr. Szabo's blog explained why he was examining these issues with such passion: The global financial crisis then underway suggested to him that the monetary system was broken and in need of replacement.

"For those who love our once and future freedoms, now is the time to strike," Mr. Szabo wrote in an item on his blog in late 2007 endorsing the libertarian Ron Paul's bid for the presidency, in part because of Mr. Paul's views on the financial system.

For many Bitcoin watchers, just as notable as what Mr. Szabo wrote in that period was his silence once Bitcoin appeared in October 2008. After all, the virtual currency was an experiment in everything he had been writing about for years. Unlike Mr. Dai, Mr. Finney and Mr. Back, Mr. Szabo has not released any correspondence from Satoshi from this period or acknowledged communicating with him.

Mr. Szabo first made brief mention of Bitcoin on his blog in mid-2009, and in 2011, when the currency was still struggling to gain traction, he wrote about it again at greater length, noting the similarity between bit gold and Bitcoin. He acknowledged that few people would have had the expertise and the instinct to create either of them:

"Myself, Wei Dai and Hal Finney were the only people I know of who liked the idea (or in Dai's case his related idea) enough to pursue it to any significant extent until Nakamoto (assuming Nakamoto is not really Finney or Dai)."

That item, in May 2011, was one of the last posts Mr. Szabo made before he went on a lengthy hiatus to work, he said later, on a new concept he called temporal programming.

May 2011 was also the last time Satoshi communicated privately with other Bitcoin contributors. In an email that month to Martti Malmi, one of the earliest participants, Satoshi wrote, "I've moved on to other things and probably won't be around in the future."

Whoever it is, the real Satoshi Nakamoto has many good reasons for wanting to stay anonymous. Perhaps the most obvious is potential danger. Sergio Demian Lerner, an Argentine researcher, has concluded that Satoshi Nakamoto most likely collected nearly a million Bitcoins during the system's first year. Given that each Bitcoin is now worth about $240, the stash could be worth more than $200 million. That could make Satoshi a target.

With his modest clothes and unassuming manner, Mr. Szabo could be the kind of person who could have a fortune and not spend any of it — or even throw away the keys to the bank. People who know him say he drives a car from the 1990s.

That modest outward appearance hasn't diminished the deference toward him among Bitcoin cognoscenti. Potential employees were drawn to Vaurum when they heard that Mr. Szabo worked there, people who interviewed at the company said. They wanted to work alongside the person they suspected could be Satoshi Nakamoto — or who at least participated in Bitcoin's invention.

CHAPTER 2

Anonymous Crime, Data Breaches and Coming Regulations

Bitcoin first thrived in the shadows. One of the first widespread sites where the digital currency was adopted was the Silk Road, an illicit deep web clearinghouse for illegal goods and services. Though the Silk Road was shut down, the seedy reputation of cryptocurrencies endured due to high-profile Bitcoin thefts and frauds. Designed to be decentralized and unregulated, cryptocurrencies attracted increasing calls for regulation and fierce debate over the integrity of the original vision.

Anonymous Payment Schemes Thriving on Web

BY NICOLE PERLROTH | MAY 29, 2013

SAN FRANCISCO — Eight years ago, Ernie Allen, the head of the International Center for Missing and Exploited Children, called the heads of major banks and credit card companies. Why, he wanted to know, were they letting child pornographers move illicit profits through their systems?

And so began a collaboration between his organization, major banks, credit card companies, Internet service providers, payment processors, and Internet companies like Google and Microsoft. They had hoped to follow the money and quash child pornography for good.

But at some point the money trail went cold. For the last year, Mr. Allen has been working with global law enforcement and financial leaders to find out why.

He may be getting closer to an answer. Today, cybersecurity experts say billions of dollars made from child pornography and illicit sales of things like national secrets and drugs are being moved through anonymous Internet payment systems like Liberty Reserve, the currency exchange whose operators were indicted Tuesday for laundering $6 billion. Preet Bharara, the United States attorney in Manhattan, described it as the largest online money-laundering case in history.

"What we have concluded is that illegal enterprises — commercial child pornography, human trafficking, drug trafficking, weapons trafficking and organized crime — has largely moved to an unregulated system that is not connected to any central bank or national authority," Mr. Allen said. "The key to all of this has been anonymity."

Liberty Reserve was shut down last weekend, but cybersecurity experts said it was just one among hundreds of anonymous Internet payment systems. They said online systems like the Moscow-based WebMoney, Perfect Money, based in Panama, and CashU, which serves the Middle East and North Africa, require little more than a valid e-mail address to initiate an account. The names and locations of the actual users are unknown and can be easily fabricated. And they worry that the no-questions-asked verification system has created a safe harbor for illicit activity.

"There are a multitude of anonymous payment systems out there, similar to Liberty Reserve, of which there are over one hundred," said Tom Kellermann, a vice president at the security company Trend Micro. "Many pretend to 'know your customer' but do not actually do due diligence."

Representatives for WebMoney, Perfect Money and CashU did not return e-mailed requests for comment.

Currency exchanges like Liberty Reserve do not take or make

Preet Bharara announced the Liberty Reserve charges.

payments of actual cash directly. Instead, they work with third parties that take payments and, in turn, credit the Liberty Reserve account.

After the authorities went after Liberty Reserve, underground forums buzzed with comments from people mourning the potential loss of frozen funds and others offering alternatives, including Bitcoin, the peer-to-peer payment network started in 2009 to offer a decentralized way to create and transfer electronic cash around the world.

In closed underground Russian-language forums, one person wrote, "I had almost 6k there. Where to now?" Another suggested, "Maybe another alternative is Perfect Money? I wonder if Bitcoin exchange rate will go up or not."

Indeed, the value of the Bitcoin virtual currency spiked temporarily on news of the Liberty Reserve shutdown. But law enforcement officials say Liberty Reserve operated with more anonymity than Bitcoin. Unlike Liberty Reserve and other anonymous payment systems, Bitcoin transactions are stored in a public ledger, called a block chain, that make it possible to trace Bitcoin transactions even years after the fact.

"You can track specific Bitcoin movements just as you would the serial number on a U.S. dollar," said Jeff Garzik, a Bitcoin developer. The real concern, security experts say, are private payment services that claim to do due diligence, but do not do even the most basic verification.

Typically, money transfers are subject to strict regulation, which include maintaining customer identification records, filing suspicious activity reports, mandatory reporting on large currency transfers, and "know-your-customer requirements." But security experts say there are a multitude of anonymous payment systems that require no customer identification and have little capability to detect or report suspicious activities.

"You would think they would be regulated but there is no regulation," Mr. Kellermann said.

Of online payment processors, PayPal is considered the gold standard. The company, now owned by eBay, has payment experts to ensure PayPal is compliant with "know-your-customer" regulations and with law enforcement agencies in each country in which it operates.

"It's unfortunate that as many of these new services come on board, it's the people looking to abuse them who are the first to use them," said Anuj Nayar, a spokesman at PayPal. "There's a lot more than just having the right technology in place to be an efficient global payment processor."

In March, the Treasury Department's Financial Crimes Enforcement Network, or FinCen, began applying anti-money laundering rules to virtual currencies, amid worries that new forms of cash purchased on the Web, like Bitcoin, were being used to finance illicit enterprises.

While Bitcoin is just a software system, there are multiple gateways and exchange points that allow Bitcoin owners to exchange their Bitcoins for cash. Federal authorities recently seized accounts associated with a United States intermediary of Mt. Gox, the world's largest Bitcoin exchange, because it was not FinCen compliant. That, and other exchanges in the United States are now racing to be fully compliant with "know-your-customer laws" and anti-money laundering requirements.

Mr. Allen said he believed that was a good first step.

"With anonymous payment systems, tracking has become virtually impossible," he said. "How do you prevent these kinds of problems when you are dealing with an unregulated currency, monitored by nobody? The answer, I think, is there has to be some kind of structure."

Disruptions: A Digital Underworld Cloaked in Anonymity

BY NICK BILTON | NOV. 17, 2013

SAN FRANCISCO — So this is where they collared the man they call the Dread Pirate Roberts.

It's up a flight of stone steps, past the circulation desk and the Romance stacks, over in Science Fiction, far corner.

On a sunny Tuesday in October, federal officers entered the public library in the Glen Park section of this city and arrested a young man who they say ran a vast Internet black market — an eBay of illegal drugs.

Their mark, Ross William Ulbricht, says he is not the F.B.I.'s Dread Pirate Roberts, the nom de guerre of the mastermind behind the marketplace, Silk Road. And the facts, his lawyer says, will prove that.

However this story plays out, Silk Road already stands as a tabloid monument to old-fashioned vice and new-fashioned technology. Until the website was shut down last month, it was the place to score, say, a brick of cocaine with a few anonymous strokes on a computer keyboard. According to the authorities, it greased $1.2 billion in drug deals and other crimes, including murder for hire.

That this story intruded here, at a public library in a nice little neighborhood, says a lot about the dark corners of the Internet. Glen Park isn't the gritty Tenderloin over the hills, or Oakland or Richmond out in East Bay. And that is precisely the point. The Dark Web, as it is known, is everywhere and nowhere, and it's growing fast.

No sooner was the old Silk Road shut down than a new, supposedly improved Silk Road popped up. Other online bazaars for illegal guns and drugs are thriving. And the Dread Pirate Roberts — the old one, a new one, who knows? — is back, taunting the authorities. (The pseudonym is a reference to a character in the film "The Princess Bride" who turns out to be not one man but rather many men passing down the title.)

The public library in the Glen Park section of San Francisco, where Ross Ulbricht, a 29-year-old software engineer, was arrested by federal agents. He is accused of running Silk Road, an Internet black market, under the pseudonym Dread Pirate Roberts.

"It took the F.B.I. two and a half years to do what they did," the Dread Pirate Roberts wrote last week on the new Silk Road site. "But four weeks of temporary silence is all they got."

So catch us if you can, the Dread Pirate is saying. The new Silk Road has overhauled its security and "marks the dawn of a brand new era for hidden services," he wrote.

The question is, can anyone really stamp out the Dread Pirates? Like the rest of the Internet, the Dark Web is being shaped and reshaped by technological innovation.

First, there was Tor, short for The Onion Router, a suite of software and network computers that enables online anonymity. Edward J. Snowden used Tor to leak government secrets, and the network has been important for dissidents in places like Iran and Egypt. Of course, drug dealers and gunrunners prefer anonymity, too.

Then there is Bitcoin, the cryptocurrency that has been sky-rocketing in value lately. Bitcoin is basically virtual cash — anonymous, untraceable currency stuffed into a mobile wallet. The kind of thing that comes in handy when buying contraband.

It's hardly news that there are bad actors on the Internet. People have been hacking this and stealing that for years. But the growth of the Dark Web is starting to attract attention in Washington. Senator Thomas R. Carper, the Delaware Democrat who is chairman of the Committee on Homeland Security and Governmental Affairs, warned recently that the authorities seemed to be playing Whac-a-Mole with websites like Silk Road. As soon as they hit one, up pops another. This, the senator said, "underscores the inescapable reality that technology is dynamic and ever-evolving and that government policy needs to adapt accordingly."

The F.B.I. declined to discuss the Silk Road case. But some security experts wonder how authorities can effectively police the Walter Whites of the web. Matthew D. Green, a research professor of computer science at Johns Hopkins, says buying illegal drugs online is now easier than buying them on the street corner. Mr. Green says that Tor is incredibly difficult to crack, but that what is really driving all this is digital cash like Bitcoin.

"And cash, in small sums, is completely untraceable," he said.

Hsinchun Chen, the director of the Artificial Intelligence Laboratory at the University of Arizona, told me that the situation was getting worse, and that there had been a rapid rise in the last few years. Mr. Chen has done research on the Dark Web and found that programmers use a vast network to trade software for drugs and other contraband. Many of these sites are set up so they can be replicated quickly if authorities take them offline.

"This underground has grown so widespread in recent years that entire international virtual communities and black markets have been spawned across the Internet to help facilitate trade between cyber criminals scattered in different parts of the world," Mr. Chen said.

How many Silk Roads are out there? No one really knows. Silk Road claimed to have one million registered users worldwide. Another site, Black Market Reloaded, advertises illegal semiautomatic handguns and AR-15-style rifles. A third, Atlantis, specializes in prescription pills. And after the original Silk Road was shut down, Sheep Marketplace, which sells weapons, drugs and counterfeit documents, quickly rose in popularity, according to Forbes.

Parmy Olson, the author of "We Are Anonymous: Inside the Hacker World of LulzSec, Anonymous, and the Global Cyber Insurgency," said that it was difficult to spot the criminals and troublemakers of the web in the real world. The bad guys on the Internet do not look like the bad guys we know, she said.

After Jake Davis, the young hacker known as Topiary, was arrested in the Shetland Islands of Scotland in 2011, Ms. Olson flew over to meet him. Mr. Davis, who worked for Anonymous, LulzSec and other groups, eventually pleaded guilty to attacks on several sites.

He was nothing like she expected. "He was just a scruffy and shy teenager," Ms. Olson said. And there are plenty of people like him — or the Dread Pirate Roberts — ready to step in and fill their shoes.

Bitcoin Scandal Reflects Popularity of Virtual Currency in China

BY ADAM CENTURY | NOV. 17, 2013

ON OCT. 26, the website of Global Bond Limited, a Chinese exchange platform for bitcoins, the booming digital currency, suddenly went dead. Then, without warning, GBL's roughly 500 remaining investors were kicked out of the company's official QQ group, a social media platform that the company was using for investor relations. By nightfall, the scale of the swindle was made public — 25 million renminbi, or $4.1 million — making it one of the largest Bitcoin fraud cases since the currency's inception four years ago.

"We want to find the culprits and make them return our hard-earned, sweat-stained money!" read one post by a victim on Sina Weibo, China's most popular Twitter-like microblog. "Help us find the criminals!"

In hindsight, there were numerous red flags that should have alerted GBL's bamboozled investors. On May 27, just days after GBL was founded, a popular Chinese Bitcoin forum pointed out that the company claimed to be based in Hong Kong, but in fact was using servers located in Beijing. In addition, GBL lacked an official company email address and did not have a license to provide financial services.

The willingness to invest in GBL despite its shortcomings demonstrates just how popular "crypto-currency" has become in China. In early November, BTC China overtook Mt. Gox and Bistamp to become the largest Bitcoin exchange site in the world, handling 34 percent of global Bitcoin transactions over the previous seven days, according to data from Bitcoinity.org, a website that tracks Bitcoin exchanges.

Bitcoin's appeal to Chinese investors is manifold. The currency experienced a major spike in value in July shortly after being the subject of overwhelmingly favorable reports on CCTV, China's state-run television station, and People's Daily, the main Communist Party newspaper. The currency received a further boost in October when the Chinese search engine Baidu, which commands more than 80 percent of the Chinese search market, announced a plan to accept bitcoins as payment for its online security and firewall services.

Last week, a real estate developer in Shanghai declared that it would accept bitcoins as payment for housing units in the city's Pudong district. The company, Shanda Tiandi, posts Bitcoin exchange values daily outside its office. This raises the possibility that China's high-net-worth investors could try to use bitcoins to circumvent strict investment caps on the property market.

Analysts say that there is a deeper and more contentious reason for China's Bitcoin boom. The popularity of the digital currency has been linked to the fact that China's citizens are unable to trade the renminbi as freely as people in other countries trade their own currencies. Beijing keeps a close grip on the renminbi, concerned about potential disruptions to the economy that could result from sudden outflows or inflows of funds.

Should the government decide to crack down on the Bitcoin, which some experts say is possible in the aftermath of such a major fraud case, it has the legal grounds to do so. In 2009, the Ministry of Commerce and the Ministry of Culture issued a rule prohibiting the exchange of virtual currency for renminbi, as well as the purchase of real-world goods and services with virtual currency.

According to sources within the tech industry, the 2009 rule was aimed mainly at companies like Tencent Holdings — the parent company of the above-mentioned QQ platform — that allow online game players to use virtual currency to purchase virtual items. But the backbone of the rule is clear: <u>Virtual currencies must stay out of the real economy.</u>

Apparent Theft at Mt. Gox Shakes Bitcoin World

BY NATHANIEL POPPER AND RACHEL ABRAMS | FEB. 25, 2014

THE MOST PROMINENT Bitcoin exchange appeared to be on the verge of collapse late Monday, raising questions about the future of a volatile marketplace.

On Monday night, a number of leading Bitcoin companies jointly announced that Mt. Gox, the largest exchange for most of Bitcoin's existence, was planning to file for bankruptcy after months of technological problems and what appeared to have been a major theft. A document circulating widely in the Bitcoin world said the company had lost 744,000 Bitcoins in a theft that had gone unnoticed for years. That would be about 6 percent of the 12.4 million Bitcoins in circulation.

While Mt. Gox did not respond to numerous requests for comments, and the companies issuing the statement scrambled to determine the exact situation at Mt. Gox, which is based in Japan, the news helped push the price of a single Bitcoin below $500 for the first time since November, when it began a spike that took it above $1,200.

But at the same time that the news about Mt. Gox was emerging, a New York firm announced plans to create an exchange that could draw the world's largest banks into the virtual currency market for the first time.

The new exchange is being put together by SecondMarket, which rose to fame a few years ago after creating a platform for buying and selling shares of companies like Twitter and Facebook before they went public.

Without the trouble at Mt. Gox, the SecondMarket plans would have been seen as a major boon for virtual currencies, providing a potential entry point into the Bitcoin market for large banks, which have so far avoided virtual currencies as their price has skyrocketed.

Barry Silbert, SecondMarket's chief executive, said that he had already talked with several banks and financial companies about joining the new exchange, along with financial regulators, and that he hoped to have it in operation this summer.

But plans for any new venture will be tested by the collapse of Mt. Gox, which could shake the faith of early Bitcoin adopters. Ryan Galt, a blogger who writes frequently about Bitcoin and was one of the first to circulate the news about Mt. Gox, wrote on Monday: "I do believe that this is one of the existential threats to Bitcoin that many have feared and have personally sold all of my Bitcoin holdings."

On Monday, Mt. Gox took down all of its previous posts on Twitter, one day after its chief executive, Mark Karpeles, resigned from the board of the Bitcoin Foundation, a nonprofit that advocates for virtual currencies.

A statement from the chief executives of Bitcoin companies like Coinbase, Circle, Blockchain.info and Payward, said that the "tragic violation of the trust of users of Mt. Gox was the result of one company's abhorrent actions and does not reflect the resilience or value of Bitcoin and the digital currency industry."

The events are in keeping with the stark ups and downs of Bitcoin's short existence.

Released in 2009 by an anonymous creator known as Satoshi Nakamoto, the Bitcoin program runs on the computers of anyone who joins in, and it is set to release only 21 million coins in regular increments. The coins can be moved between digital wallets using secret passwords.

While Bitcoin fans have said the technology could provide a revolutionary new way of moving money around the world, skeptics have viewed it variously as a Ponzi scheme or an investment susceptible to fraud and theft.

Many leading names in the Bitcoin community were still trying to determine the scope and potential consequences of the troubles at Mt. Gox. A document detailing the purported theft, labeled "Crisis Strategy Draft," appeared to come from Mt. Gox.

While officials at the Bitcoin Foundation could not verify the origins of the document, they were preparing for the closure of Mt. Gox.

Patrick Murck, the foundation's general counsel, said that "this incident just demonstrates the need for initiatives by responsible individuals and responsible members of the Bitcoin community like what's being described" in SecondMarket's initiative.

Mt. Gox's difficulties this week are only the latest in a long line of problems at the Tokyo-based exchange. Created in 2010, Mt. Gox quickly became the most popular place to buy and sell Bitcoins. But the firm has suffered several intrusions and technological mishaps, which have led to steep declines in the currency's price. A few weeks ago the company stopped allowing its customers to withdraw Bitcoins after it said it had discovered a flaw in some of the basic Bitcoin computer code.

While other exchanges were briefly hit by problems, they came back online. Mt. Gox never opened up again, prompting speculation about its future.

Until now, the major Bitcoin exchanges have all allowed anyone from the public to buy and sell virtual currency. SecondMarket's plan is to create a platform more like the New York Stock Exchange, where only large institutions can join and trade.

Mr. Silbert says he will only open the exchange once they have several regulated financial institutions signed on as members. His hope, he says, is to give them partial ownership so that they have an incentive to trade there.

For much of Bitcoin's life, banks have viewed the virtual currency with either derision or dismissiveness.

Recently, though, a number of banks have released research reports that have been less negative. A December report from Bank of America said that virtual currencies could become an important new part of the payment system, allowing money to move more cheaply than it does with credit cards and money transmitters like Western Union.

The statement from the Bitcoin companies on Monday night, which was not signed by Mr. Silbert, said that "in order to re-establish the trust squandered by the failings of Mt. Gox, responsible Bitcoin exchanges are working together and are committed to the future of Bitcoin and the security of all customer funds."

Bitcoin Is Not Yet Ready for the Real World

BY MARK T. WILLIAMS | JAN. 24, 2014

IT IS UNDERSTANDABLE why some in the venture capital sector are over the moon about Bitcoin and its endless possibilities. Marc Andreessen of Andreessen Horowitz has about 50 million reasons why he wants Bitcoin to succeed. The only problem is that Bitcoin is a concept dreamed up in the virtual world and is not yet ready for the real world.

Bitcoin technology and its lower-cost payment system design may be elegant but that does not mean it should be blindly embraced and adopted. The payment system and Bitcoin as an e-currency can't be divorced from each other. Before Bitcoin becomes a regular and reliable method for consumer transactions, several significant risks need to be assessed and addressed:

REPUTATIONAL RISK

Is Bitcoin an innovative response to facilitate meaningful commerce or simply a designer currency for the criminally inclined? For Bitcoin to function as a currency, it has to be trusted as an honest means for transacting business. Its reputation needs to be rock solid.

Since its inception, Bitcoin has been a decentralized experiment with a morphing purpose. In 2009, in response to the Great Recession, Bitcoin was seen as a way to take back control from irresponsible central bankers, reallocating power of currency to the people through computer code and a decentralized payment system. However, creating an unregulated and untraceable currency also made it the currency of choice for those engaged in illicit activities.

The F.B.I.'s takedown of Silk Road in October 2013 significantly tarnished Bitcoin's reputation by exposing a deep web of drugs, guns, prostitution, assassins for hire and a ready tool for tax evasion and money laundering.

TROJAN HORSE RISK

For the last five years, the pseudo name of Satoshi Nakamoto has been used to symbolize the innovative genius (or team) behind Bitcoin. Given that Bitcoin has mushroomed to $10 billion in value and prospects for commercialization abound, it is puzzling why this supposed e-currency messiah has not stepped forward. What if Satoshi Nakamoto is not real, and his likeness was manufactured by some cyber-criminals to generate investor excitement?

At this embryonic stage it seems only logical that the true spokesman, not just someone from the venture capital industry, should step forward to part the waters, lead the followers and show the way. Or at least be the industry face before the growing number of e-currency regulatory hearings that will help shape industry economics and future prospects.

Could it be that this coding genius is instead enjoying computer-manufactured riches on some remote, tax-free island, or is he a cyber-terrorist who upon Bitcoin adoption will activate a Trojan-horse virus to bring world commerce back to the Stone Age?

ASSET BUBBLE RISK

The speculative mania generated around Bitcoin has created a hyper asset bubble that is ready to pop. Since 2013, Bitcoin has risen from $13 to as high as $1,200 with price appreciation of more than 9,000 percent. There are 12.3 million coins outstanding, over 90 percent are hoarded, which helps to artificially inflate values.

Ownership is also extremely concentrated, increasing market manipulation risk. As prices have grown to the clouds, many Bitcoin millionaires have been minted along the way. But what supports these lofty prices?

Bitcoin is neither a legal entity, nor a start-up, and no stock is available for investors to purchase. It has no management team, board, balance sheet, business plan or even a coherent vision on how to commercialize technology that has been given away in the market for free. Even Mr. Andreessen, the venture capitalist, disclosed that he held only a de minimis amount of Bitcoin, making it clear that smart money is not betting on e-coins but directly on Bitcoin-related start-ups.

Increasingly, as Bitcoin investors gain greater awareness of what they actually bought (and more important not bought), values will fall further. In the last month, Bitcoin has dropped by about 30 percent. The bursting of the Bitcoin bubble will put in jeopardy the viability of the lauded payment system as it can't be easily separated from the use of Bitcoin as its currency.

CONSUMER AND INVESTOR PROTECTION RISK

Bitcoin is built around an unregulated, decentralized and untraceable coin. No legal protection is in place to assist consumers or investors.

If a consumer were to send a Bitcoin to the wrong e-wallet, if a hard drive storing coins were corrupted (intentionally or unintentionally), or an e-wallet picked, coin value is lost forever. The chance of counterfeiting increases as the profit potential has risen. Already, of the e-coins outstanding, an estimated 4 percent, or $400 million, have been permanently lost.

As Bitcoin's value has skyrocketed, the amount of fraud related to stolen coins has increased. Recently, it was reported that $220 million in coins were stolen and not recovered. It is hard to track fraudulent activities and those who perpetrate these acts because e-coins are untraceable. For Bitcoin to work and protect consumers and investors, there needs to be clear legal protection. This will have to be implemented on a nation-by-nation basis with international cooperation. Without it, unacceptably high risk will persist and limit adoption.

REGULATORY RISK

Bitcoin's rapid price climb and growing visibility has also been its greatest weakness. In the last month, some of the world's wealthiest nations have realized there are numerous risks like economic instability that Bitcoin could pose if it is not properly regulated.

There are a growing number of nations that have begun to debunk the idea it could serve as a real currency. China, the second-largest economy in the world, announced in December that it would not accept Bitcoin, and within 48 hours the price dropped as much as 50 percent. Other influential nations and authorities have also spoken out against Bitcoin, including Denmark, Finland, France, India, Norway, Sweden, Thailand and the European Banking Authority.

Next week, the New York State Department of Financial Services will hold an important hearing to further help clarify the role that Bitcoin should or should not play as it relates to our financial sector. Under this growing regulatory climate and concerns about not being able to prevent money laundering, American commercial banks are hesitant to open accounts with Bitcoin-related start-ups.

Increasingly, the fate of the commercial viability of e-currencies is moving into the hands of nations, their regulators and financial protectors and out of the control of Bitcoin enthusiasts.

MARK T. WILLIAMS, a former commodities trading floor senior executive and Federal Reserve Bank examiner, teaches banking, finance and risk management at Boston University School of Management.

To Instill Love of Bitcoin, Backers Work to Make It Safe

BY NICOLE PERLROTH | APRIL 1, 2014

SAN FRANCISCO — Bitcoin's future may not rely on stabilizing its price swings or signing up more merchants to accept the virtual currency. Rather, it may rely on its image.

In the last few months, the value of Bitcoin has been cut in half, in the face of questions about security issues and concerns about new regulations.

Warren E. Buffett referred to the currency as a "mirage" in an interview last month and told people to "stay away." Would-be adopters and investors have grown fearful as hackers develop new ways to steal Bitcoin and major Bitcoin exchanges shut down. The Internal Revenue Service has even weighed in on how Bitcoin will be taxed.

Proponents have a mounting public relations crisis on their hands, particularly as Bitcoin becomes hackers' preferred payment method. Hackers have recently taken to mounting large scale denial-of-service attacks on tech start-ups — most recently, Meetup, a social meeting site; Vimeo, the video sharing service; and Basecamp, a project management software company — and demanding payments via Bitcoin as ransom to cease.

Even the Bitcoin Foundation, a nonprofit group that was set up to promote Bitcoin's legitimate use, was marred after one of its board members was arrested and charged with money laundering.

In fact, the biggest Bitcoin holder is the United States government, after the F.B.I. seized some 144,000 coins — roughly $66 million at current prices — from Silk Road, the now-defunct digital market that prosecutors say aided drug deals and other illicit transactions.

Consumer confidence in and adoption of new technologies — especially regarding money — is highly dependent on security, or at least the public's perception of security. To that end, Bitcoin enthusiasts, cryptographers and security researchers are putting renewed focus on security and self-policing.

They face an uphill battle. While the Bitcoin system itself is protected by strong cryptography, thieves have pilfered hundreds of millions of dollars' worth of coins by exploiting weaknesses in private key storage systems and hundreds of millions more from exchanges.

Joe Stewart and Pat Litke, two security researchers at Dell Secure-Works, set out in recent months to evaluate the threats facing Bitcoin. They discovered more than 120 unique families of malware on the Internet that had been specifically engineered to steal Bitcoin wallet files from people's computers, or to steal coins through other means such as recording a user's keystrokes so an attacker could grab a user's private keys as they type them in.

The most common strains of malware they discovered were so-called wallet stealers, software specifically designed to search for a user's Bitcoin wallet on a hard drive or in well-known file locations. The attackers would then upload the information to a remote server, extract the keys and steal coins.

Security experts have long advised the use of long, secure passwords, but Mr. Litke and Mr. Stewart found that in some cases, the attackers managed to bypass strong passcodes by using a keylogger, which records passwords when victims type them in, or by monitoring the copy-and-paste clipboard function.

When the researchers tested the cryptocurrency malware against popular antivirus systems, they found the average detection rate was an abysmal 48.9 percent. More than half of major antivirus solutions failed to detect attackers' malicious code. And, unlike cases of credit card fraud, in which credit card companies can reimburse the victims, Bitcoin theft is similar to theft of cash. Once it's gone, it's probably gone for good.

"It's incredibly easy for malware to steal Bitcoin, especially if you're keeping them on the same computer you use to casually browse the Internet," Mr. Stewart said. "There are so many holes for criminals to walk through."

Mr. Stewart and other security researchers now advise users to keep their Bitcoin in so-called cold storage. The private keys needed to conduct a transaction are stored on a secure offline device, or even printed out, much like storing the bulk of one's cash in a physical safe.

Some of the biggest Bitcoin thefts have occurred at the exchanges. Mt. Gox's operators say hackers were able to steal more than $450 million worth of Bitcoin using a bug that tricked its system into moving a user's coins to an attacker's account, while simultaneously fooling Mt. Gox's system into thinking the withdrawal did not go through.

Mt. Gox would then resend the requested amount, effectively doubling the withdrawal from a user's account. Mt. Gox asserted that hackers used this bug to make off with 850,000 coins — 750,000 owned by customers and 100,000 owned by Mt. Gox at the time of the announcement. One month later, Mark Karpeles, Mt. Gox's 28-year-old chief executive, said the company had found 200,000 coins in an old wallet.

But last week, two Swiss researchers compared Mt. Gox's assertions with what they had witnessed across Bitcoin's distributed network. By creating specialized nodes that could trace and dump all transactions across the Bitcoin network, they found that only 386 coins could have been successfully stolen from the Bitcoin network using the bug Mt. Gox cited. Their conclusion: Some 650,000 coins were unaccounted for.

Representatives for Mt. Gox did not return requests for comment. But after Mt. Gox was shut down in late February, other prominent exchanges were suddenly attacked. Flexcoin said it was hacked on March 2, forcing it to shut down. On March 5, Crypto-Trade also said it was attacked, but recently said it had resumed allowing Bitcoin withdrawals. To avoid similar fates, Bitcoin proponents, researchers and exchanges have started new systems and self-regulations to help instill confidence among adopters and bring Bitcoin into mainstream use.

Two programmers from the Czech Republic, Marek Palatinus and Pavol Ruznak, created the Trezor Wallet after Mr. Palatinus lost more than 3,000 coins to cyberthieves. The wallet, a hardware device that cannot be infected by malware, makes cold storage more practical. A new Bitcoin vault service, Xapo, is promising to insure deposits from any losses to hacker attacks, theft by a Xapo employee, break-ins at its vault or any bankruptcy.

Elsewhere, exchanges are working to improve "transaction integrity verification," or the system by which transactions can be tied back to identities. An initiative called the Bison Network — or the Bitcoin Identity Security Open Network — is working with Jumio, a four-year-old credential management company backed by Andreessen Horowitz, the venture capital firm, to validate buyer's identities using Jumio's software.

And after the I.R.S. announced last week that Bitcoin would be considered property and taxed as such, media reports pointed out that those living in the United States would have to begin the onerous task of tracking their Bitcoin purchases, or risk submitting fraudulent tax returns. Customers of Overstock, for example, may need accountants to figure out capital gains taxes on all the ups and downs of their Bitcoin holdings if they use the virtual currency every time they buy furniture on the site.

The worry, many say, is that mounting security and a proliferation of rules could mean death by a thousand cuts. Max Levchin, a co-founder of PayPal, the digital payment system that itself was the target for hackers before it achieved acceptance, said in an interview this week that Bitcoin's fate would ultimately be dictated by whether users could find the right balance between security and convenience.

"What is slowing down adoption is that Bitcoin can be hard to understand and hard to use," Mr. Levchin said. "It has to get really simple. For that simplicity to really happen, most often it necessarily has to become less secure to become more convenient."

"But at PayPal," Mr. Levchin added. "I'd like to claim we found the intersection. So I know it's doable."

As Bitcoin Bubble Loses Air, Frauds and Flaws Rise to Surface

BY NATHANIEL POPPER | FEB. 5, 2018

SAN FRANCISCO — You did not have to be a technophobe to worry that the virtual-currency boom of the past year papered over plenty of problems.

The scale of those problems is starting to become clear as digital tokens have slid more than 50 percent in value from their peaks in early January, with steep drops on Monday pushing the value of Bitcoin specifically below $7,000.

Hackers draining funds from online exchanges. Ponzi schemes. Government regulators unable to keep up with the rise of so-called cryptocurrencies. Signs of trouble have appeared at nearly every level of the industry, from the biggest exchanges to the news sites and chat rooms where the investment frenzy has been discussed.

On Tuesday, the leaders of the two main regulatory agencies in the United States that oversee the technology, the Securities and Exchange Commission and the Commodity Futures Trading Commission, are to testify before the Senate banking committee about their efforts to police virtual currency markets. In the past two weeks, both have brought major cases, but people in the young industry said regulators had barely made a dent.

Some virtual currency enthusiasts argue that the problems are no different from what has happened in other booms, like the internet bubble of the 1990s. But even true believers say the design of virtual currencies — meant to cut out middlemen and government authorities — has made bad behavior more prevalent amid this particular bubble.

"Cryptocurrencies are almost a perfect vehicle for scams," said Kevin Werbach, a professor at University of Pennsylvania's Wharton School. "The combination of credulous buyers and low barriers for scammers were bound to lead to a high level of fraud, if and when the money involved got large. The fact that the money got huge almost overnight, before there were good regulatory or even self-regulatory models in place, made the problem acute."

The fall from the peaks of early January has been dizzying. The value of all outstanding virtual currencies has been cut by more than half, down over $400 billion as of Monday, according to the website Coinmarketcap.com.

In January, the heads of the main regulators wrote in The Wall Street Journal that the situation presented an unprecedented challenge. "These markets are new, evolving and international," Jay Clayton, the Securities and Exchange Commission's chairman, and J. Christopher Giancarlo, his counterpart at the Commodity Futures Trading Commission, wrote. "As such they require us to be nimble and forward-looking."

Government agencies in the United States have shut down a few notable frauds. Early last month, securities regulators in Texas and North Carolina issued cease-and-desist orders to BitConnect, an operation that had grown to be worth $3 billion.

But those moves only came after BitConnect had operated openly for months, collecting hundreds of millions of dollars from people around the world despite being labeled a Ponzi scheme by many prominent people in the virtual currency industry. BitConnect offered tokens on a decentralized network, similar to Bitcoin, but promised regular payouts to coin holders.

In January, the Commodity Futures Trading Commission shut down My Big Coin, a purported swindle that had attracted $6 million.

But regulators have not gotten near most of the brazen schemes that have popped up in the past year, many of which had been attacked by hackers first, or simply shut down by their operators after money had been raised.

A new virtual currency, Proof of Weak Hands Coin, whose creators referred to it as a Ponzi scheme on Twitter and use a pyramid as a website logo, raised $800,000 before hackers got into its systems last week and drained its funds. Another pyramid scheme, MMM, which was shut down in an earlier incarnation by the Russian government, has been revived thanks to the popularity of Bitcoin and is operating openly, with particular success in Africa.

One challenge facing regulators is that it is unclear how much of the deceptive activity they can legally control.

Some online groups openly try to manipulate the prices of digital tokens in what are known as pump-and-dump schemes. Similar schemes involving stocks are illegal, but people operating the groups recently told BuzzFeed that they did not think the same rules applied to virtual currencies.

Many schemes have been able to expand quickly because they do not use bank accounts and therefore do not have to win approval from established institutions. Instead, they are able to use virtual currency "wallets" without any approvals. And virtual currency transactions cannot be reversed like normal bank or even PayPal transfers.

With regulators slow to crack down, the private sector has taken on a more important role. Facebook announced last week that it would no longer allow advertisements for virtual currency projects. On Friday, JPMorgan Chase and Bank of America said they would bar customers from using credit cards to purchase virtual currencies; Citigroup followed suit on Monday.

For investors, some of what has caused the most concern are well-intentioned businesses set up in a hurry with little outside oversight or time to work out kinks.

Coincheck, which until last month was one of the largest exchanges in Japan, announced on Jan. 26 that it had lost nearly half a billion dollars of a virtual currency known as NEM, in what appeared to be the largest hack to hit the industry.

Traders have been particularly worried about the largest Bitcoin exchange in the world, Bitfinex, an unregulated operation that has provided few details about its operations, raising concerns about whether it is insolvent or involved in price manipulation.

In the United States, even the most widely used virtual currency company, Coinbase, has struggled to keep up with demand, shutting down trading for hours at particularly important moments, and attracting widespread complaints about its customer service.

But the biggest number of incidents have cropped up around so-called initial coin offerings, in which entrepreneurs sell custom virtual currencies to investors to raise money for software they are building. About 890 projects raised over $6 billion last year, a 6,000 percent increase over the year before, according to Icodata.io, which tracks the offerings.

The $240 million raised through one of the most successful initial coin offerings last year, Tezos, is already frozen in a dispute between the founders of the project and the board they created in Switzerland.

Even established companies like Kodak have ended up chasing the riches without doing proper due diligence. The company delayed its own initial coin offering after it was revealed that the people assisting the venture had problematic histories and little relevant experience.

Most of the newer virtual currency projects borrow their basic design from Bitcoin, which uses a network of computers to maintain its records so that no central government or authority is needed.

That design has allowed Bitcoin and other virtual currencies to grow as fast as they have with no regard for international borders, attracting followers from Zimbabwe to South Korea. It has also allowed some of the most talked-about uses of the technology, helping people escape hyperinflation in Venezuela or transfer money across borders with lower fees. But it has also allowed in a lot of bad actors.

"It is a perfect storm for the kind of scammy activity we are seeing, and it's not obvious to me how that is easily removed," said Fred Wilson, a partner at the venture capital firm Union Square Venture and one of the earliest advocates of Bitcoin in Silicon Valley. "Regulation, ideally prudent and informed regulation, can help. But we may also need to have a big correction to really clean things up."

CHAPTER 3

Bitcoin Bubbles and Busts: Behind the Volatility

Cryptocurrencies have been characterized by enormous volatility, with two high-profile bubbles and busts. In 2013–2014, Bitcoin's value rose due to mainstream adoption and dropped after major thefts prompted Chinese regulation on its domestic exchanges. In 2016–2018, a fervor for competing coins drew comparisons to the tech bubble of the early 2000s, with overnight millionaires and warnings of overvalued companies. Though Bitcoin's $20,000 high fell to less than $7,000 as of summer 2018, many still speculate that the cryptocurrency values may rise again.

Bubble or No, This Virtual Currency Is a Lot of Coin in Any Realm

BY NOAM COHEN | APRIL 7, 2013

WHEN HE WAS a Yale Law School student, Reuben Grinberg wrote one of the first academic papers about Bitcoin, a novel virtual currency that uses sophisticated cryptography to validate and secure transactions that exist only online.

When Mr. Grinberg, now a lawyer in the financial institutions group of the Manhattan law firm Davis Polk & Wardwell, first learned about bitcoins, they were selling for 10 cents. Now, after the latest price surge that began in January, the cost of a Bitcoin on an exchange that converts them to dollars is something like $140, and the collective value of all bitcoins has passed a billion dollars.

That is a lot of coin in any form, and the billion-dollar milestone has turned the once-obscure online currency into a media sensation. Had Mr. Grinberg invested just $100 back then, today his investment would be worth …

Ah, but that way madness lies. "People are buying bitcoins because the price is going up," he said in an interview. "That is the classic indicator of a bubble."

The question of whether the increase represents real value or is simply evidence of a bubble is at the heart of the current media frenzy. Bitcoin began in January 2009, a project introduced by a programmer or group of programmers who worked under the name Satoshi Nakamoto.

The project represented a breakthrough in using software code to authenticate and protect transactions without resorting to a centralized bank or government treasury. In that way, Bitcoin became a peer-to-peer system. That comes in pretty handy for people who do not want their transactions monitored.

In conversations about the project with scholars who study it, the word that comes up as often as "bubble" is "genius."

For one thing, though bitcoins are software code, you can't simply copy them like a music file. The process of creating the coins — "mining" them in the project's allusion to something tangible like gold or silver — involves computer work that, crucially, verifies Bitcoin transactions.

"It is the most successful digital currency already right now," said Nicolas Christin, the associate director of the Information Networking Institute at Carnegie Mellon University. "Even if bitcoins become worth nothing, it has succeeded more than any academic proposals for a digital currency," he said in an interview from Okinawa, Japan, where he was attending a conference on financial cryptography that included a number of papers on bitcoins.

Bitbills are physical representations of the virtual currency known as Bitcoin.

People buy the coins for cold hard cash on exchanges. Completing those purchases, as well as cashing out, typically involves re-entering the world of traditional financial transactions, with fees and loss of anonymity.

But Bitcoin's managers say the currency has proved so secure that despite the fact that exchanges and virtual wallets, where people keep their bitcoins, have been hacked, the coins themselves have not been forged.

So why the sudden run-up in value? Some point to the recent crisis over Cypriot banks, which made a currency beyond the control of governments more tempting. And as with a run-up in anything tradable — tulip bulbs, dot-com shares — there is also the hypnotic logic that says the price went up today, so that means it will go up tomorrow.

Some observers and investors also make the case that bitcoins are in fact undervalued. Their argument goes like this. The total value of the world's economic activity is enormous. There are certain transactions that are ideal for bitcoins because the currency is relatively anonymous and does not need to be processed by a financial organization or a government.

If bitcoins become the dominant currency in some small niche of the world economy — that is, those people who do not want their transactions easily tracked or who want to send money back home from abroad — then they will become quite valuable indeed. This outcome has been neatly summarized by the financial blogger Felix Salmon as making bitcoins an "uncomfortable combination of commodity and currency."

The price increase becomes a question of supply and demand. Unlike other currencies that can adjust the money supply depending on economic conditions, bitcoins have a supply that is fixed. The amount of new coins that can be minted was plotted at the outset with a finite number of coins at the end, roughly 21 million in the next century. Today, the rate is 25 new coins every 10 minutes; for the first four years, it was twice as many, 50 every 10 minutes.

The slowdown in the rate new coins are added, which was programmed into bitcoins, may also help account for the spike in prices.

So far, excluding investors and day traders, the main use of the currency appears to be illicit activity. There are the online gambling sites that use bitcoins. And the anonymous online marketplace Silk Road, which accepts only bitcoins, is "overwhelmingly used as a market for controlled substances and narcotics," according to a paper on Silk Road written by Mr. Christin of Carnegie Mellon.

He used clues on the site, including buyer feedback reports, to calculate how much and what kind of business was being transacted. His conclusion, as of July 2012, was that $1.2 million in business was carried out each month, much of it for buying small amounts of narcotics that were delivered by mail. "We did see it was growing," he said of the total value of the trades. "It pretty much doubled in the six months I followed it."

Excluding the traders, he said, "Silk Road probably represents a sizable amount of Bitcoin exchanges, but not more than half."

Supporters of the Bitcoin project acknowledge these statistics but argue that it can still thrive as a mainstream currency.

"I think when you talk about Silk Road, you are talking about the first early adopter market — there is no other solution that works," said Gavin Andresen, chief scientist at the Bitcoin Foundation, a nonprofit organization that manages the project. When the currency evolves to be more useful and better known, he said, it will be used for more mundane transactions.

Even the idea that it is experiencing a bubble — and Mr. Andresen said in an interview by phone from Amherst, Mass., "I think it definitely is a frenzy" — is for the best. "Eventually the media gets bored and moves on to the next thing," he said, "and what is left behind is a whole new wave of people interested." And, he says, a much lower price for bitcoins.

As evidence of mainstream interest, Mr. Andresen pointed to the Bitcoin 2013 conference in San Jose, Calif., next month, which is attracting entrepreneurs with Silicon Valley venture capital backing. The list of panelists is heavy with start-up executives, but includes some activists — including representatives from the Web site Antiwar.com and the Electronic Frontier Foundation — who see a currency outside of government regulation as crucial to financing projects that criticize the authorities.

Mr. Andresen is not a mere bystander to the fluctuations in Bitcoin prices. As an employee of the Bitcoin Foundation, after working as a volunteer on the software, he is paid in bitcoins, with the rate set every three months. In 2013, his salary in terms of dollars has increased more than tenfold.

Starting in April, however, the foundation has decided that, because of those fluctuations, his Bitcoin salary would be adjusted each month, he said. Still, that alone makes this bubble different than many in the past: the creators are not looking to get their money and make a quick exit.

Chinese Bitcoin Investors Fret as Value of Virtual Currency Plunges

BY AUSTIN RAMZY | DEC. 19, 2013

THE VIRTUAL CURRENCY Bitcoin has taken a sharp tumble in value since Chinese regulators moved to restrict its usage. That has created no small amount of grumbling among Chinese Bitcoin buyers, who have been some of the most enthusiastic investors in the digital money.

"The drop in Bitcoin's value in the last few days has been terrible, I've felt really uncertain," an investor surnamed Chen told The Securities Times, a Chinese financial newspaper. Mr. Chen said he had bought five coins recently at a price of 3,100 renminbi, or about $510, apiece. On Wednesday the value dropped to three-quarters of that. "I thought I'd make a little short-term investment," he said. "I didn't think I'd lose money."

On Wednesday, BTC China, the country's largest Bitcoin exchange, said it had been told to stop accepting deposits in Chinese currency. The announcement was the latest in a series of steps that have restricted the ability to buy and use Bitcoins in China. The country's leading third-party payment processors were told on Monday by the central bank to stop accepting the currency, according to Chinese news reports. And on Dec. 5, the People's Bank of China and other regulators ordered traditional financial institutions in China to stop Bitcoin transactions.

Those moves have raised widespread doubts in China over the virtual currency, which saw values climb to 7,395 renminbi, or $1,218, on Dec. 1. After dropping to 2,300 renminbi late Wednesday, the price for a Bitcoin quoted by BTC China recovered slightly to around 3,000 renminbi by Thursday afternoon.

Chinese economists had warned investors about the risks inherent in the virtual money.

"When it comes to Bitcoin, early on I said that ordinary people should stay far away from it," Yi Xianrong, an economist with the Chinese Academy of Social Sciences, wrote on his Tencent Weibo microblog after the central bank began making moves to restrict Bitcoin in early December. "It's not a real currency — it doesn't have a guarantee of creditworthiness. The risks are very high, and if ordinary people play the market they're on their own. The central bank announcement told us what would happen with people who thought they were going to get rich quick and just got burned."

One Chinese Bitcoin investor bought 10 Bitcoins when the price was at 2,000 renminbi each after seeing friends earn good returns, The Economic Daily News reported. "After half a month or so the price climbed to 7,000. It was unexpected and I was so happy. But I didn't sell them. I thought, even if it dropped a little, I would still be ahead," the investor, who was identified only by the surname Xu, told the paper.

Some Chinese media outlets said the website of the People's Bank of China was inaccessible for a short period on Wednesday afternoon, and said it might have been the target of a hacking attempt launched in retaliation over the moves to restrict Bitcoin use. The Beijing Times newspaper quoted a bank representative who confirmed that the website had been down but was operating normally by 6 p.m. The bank representative offered no explanation as to the cause of the temporary problem.

Bitcoin Is a Protocol.
Bitcoin Is a Brand.

BY QUENTIN HARDY | MARCH 6, 2014

SO IT APPEARS the creator of Bitcoin may not have been a young Japanese mathematical wizard as had been long rumored. Instead, as Newsweek has first reported, he is believed to be a 64-year-old Japanese-American man named Satoshi Nakamoto who clearly does not care for attention.

It is notable that the man Newsweek has identified as the creator of Bitcoin has denied that he has anything to do with it. There is also — still — wide confusion about what Bitcoin is.

Bitcoin, an Internet-based cryptocurrency, has been in the news for months, of course. Conceptions of what Bitcoin actually is, however, still run from money to software to a network of diehard believers.

The Bitcoin-like currencies like Auroracoin, Dogecoin or Unobtanium offer another perspective: More than anything, Bitcoin is a brand.

On one level, Bitcoin is an open-source software protocol for creating an encrypted "currency," against which people store value. That is partly to give users peace of mind, since it can be inspected for security or flaws and upgraded by its own users.

Open-source code can also be copied and reconfigured, cheaply enough that you might consider making a coin for your sweetheart.

"It takes about 20 minutes, and costs about $50," said Brock Pierce, a Bitcoin entrepreneur and investor. "I've seen 275 logos of different coins. There's probably thousands." He was speaking at the Oasis conference in Los Angeles, where a crowd of traditional investors seemed generally warm to the new currencies.

There is not a lot of financial risk here. The website Coinmarketcap keeps tabs on the 100 most valuable. The biggest is Bitcoin, with a total market capitalization of about $8.3 billion, or 70 percent of the $11.1 billion in total market cap of all 100 coins.

Ripple, the second largest (and a trading system not based on Bitcoin) is at $1.5 billion. The recent No. 100 on the list, Pandacoin, had a market cap of $88,537, or about twice what Arby's paid for the hat that the singer Pharrell Williams wore at the Grammy awards in January.

It should be noted that the recent fall of the Mt. Gox Bitcoin exchange, with losses of about $460 million, had much more to do with the lack of oversight at the exchange, and not with Bitcoin as a protocol.

Eric E. Schmidt, the executive chairman of Google, is one believer in the integrity of the Bitcoin software. "I had a look at the code," he said. "It's very good. Very sound."

Several of the new "–coins" themselves are gimmicky. Auroracoin promises to give coins to every citizen of Iceland, and recently had the fourth-largest market cap, at $367 million. Dogecoin is named for the lovable Internet meme. Unobtanium is named after the preposterous anti-gravitational mineral in the movie "Avatar."

It pains some Bitcoin fans. "Early on, I thought, 'Oh God — fragmentation,' " Mr. Pierce said. "It's inevitable." Now he's decided that it's a good thing. Lots of people are trying out different styles of money, until the world finds one it loves.

Which shows how Bitcoin's fate is tied to its brand: The network of users is also a network of believers, who are moved to use one of these protocols over another as a currency. And if the brand falters, Bitcoin will be sold off. To that end, Bitcoin's fast recovery from the Mt. Gox collapse is a positive for the brand.

It could be argued that paper money is a country's brand, as well, except traditional money comes with hard rules and enforced regulations that tend to overpower emotional claims. Dogecoin, which became big in part because that doggie is just so cute, cannot quite make the same claim.

In open-source software, continuous tweaks to existing code, to the point of making the end product altogether different, is known as "forking." It is considered bad, since it makes it hard to build a standard.

The continual churn of currencies, and the promiscuous use of the protocol, make some people suspicious of how well Bitcoin and its kin will endure.

"I used to do security for a lot of three-letter agencies, and I don't think Bitcoin has really been through a thorough security check," said Alex Payne, co-founder and former chief technical officer of Simple, an online bank that last month was sold to BBVA for $117 million.

"A cryptocurrency that the world uses for the next 50 years will have to get audits from regulators, universities, places the entrepreneurs of these currencies like to ridicule," he added.

Grandpa Had a Pension. This Generation Has Cryptocurrency.

BY TEDDY WAYNE | AUG. 3, 2017

MOST READERS have probably heard of Bitcoin, the digital coin that dominates the cryptocurrency market. It has gained notice both because of its skyrocketing value (from less than a cent in early 2010 to around $2,600 currently) and because it is frequently a key player in hacking- and black-market-related stories, from the looting of nearly half a billion dollars in coins from the Mt. Gox exchange in 2014 to the recent demand for payment in Bitcoin in the WannaCry ransomware attack.

But do you know Ethereum, with a total value of coins in circulation of close to $20 billion? Bitcoin Cash, which split off from the original Bitcoin on Aug. 1, lost about half its value within hours, then nearly quadrupled by the next day? Or, rounding out the Big Four, Ripple — whose currency is known as XRP — which shot up to about 40 cents by mid-May from less than a cent at the end of March? (Full disclosure: I owned but unloaded three of these currencies before writing this article.) Then there are over 800 lower-value and often creatively named coins among those listed on Coinmarketcap.com. One can buy FedoraCoin (its jaunty symbol being the Justin Timberlake-approved hat), CannabisCoin (one guess what it looks like) or, to choose one of many bringing up the rear, Quartz, currently priced around three-thousandths of a cent. (Bad news for those who bought it at just under $2 at the end of May.)

After years as a niche market for technologically sophisticated anarchists and libertarians excited about a decentralized financial network not under government control, digital coins may be on the verge of going mainstream. "It's the wild, wild West," said Ron Ginn, 35, founder of a private photo-sharing service called Text Event Pics in St. Augustine, Fla., who has taken all his money out of the stock market and put it into Ripple and real estate. "This is like getting to invest in the internet in the '90s. I'm obviously very bullish, but I expect to make a couple million dollars off very little money. This is the opportunity of a lifetime. Finance is getting its internet."

Cryptocurrency has understandable appeal to millennials who came of age during the 2008 financial crisis and are now watching the rise of antiglobalist populism threaten the stability of the international economy.

"There's a low cost for entry, you don't pay a lot of fees and millennials are the most tech-savvy," said John Guarco, 22, a recent Duke graduate living on Staten Island who, like most of the people interviewed for this article, asked that names of the coins in which he has invested not be published for fear of being targeted by hackers.

Unlike previous generations, many of these greenhorn investors don't have pensions or 401(k)'s, are mistrustful of socking money away in mutual funds and are fully accustomed to owning digital assets that have no concrete properties. As traditional paths to upper-middle-class stability are being blocked by debt, exorbitant housing costs and a shaky job market, these investors view cryptocurrency not only as a hedge against another Dow Jones crash, but also as the most rational — and even utopian — means of investing their money.

Sebastian Dinges, 33, the director of operations for Cheeky, a company that makes mealtime products, started his first job after college in 2007. Once he had enough money to invest in the stock market, he said, he "wanted to be risky and get a big return." Within six months, the market crashed.

"So there's definitely disillusionment," he said.

The majority of Mr. Dinges's holdings are now in cryptocurrency. His skepticism of traditional markets is shared by a number of cryptocurrency enthusiasts in his age bracket who have observed the recent political and economic upheavals.

"I do feel we've reached a new level where nobody knows what's going to happen," said Gabe Wax, 24, who runs the Rare Book Room recording studio in Brooklyn. "The things we've been able to rely on aren't as reliable and we have a president who knows absolutely nothing about how the economy works, and he's appointed people who have twisted views about how it works. That, more than anything, is what scares me."

Mr. Wax was still in high school when the 2008 crisis unfolded, but he was paying attention to the headlines. So was Mr. Guarco, who said cryptocurrency was a "safeguard against the volatility in the rest of the world."

"Investing in cryptocurrencies is a hedge," he continued. "We're entering a period of long-term deregulation and tax cuts to the wealthiest. It's not the best recipe for stability."

Mr. Wax also invests in cryptocurrency to shore up his finances as a freelancer in the precarious music industry.

"I constantly feel like I'm looking over the edge of a cliff," he said. "I don't like the idea of money just sitting in a savings account — with the way inflation works and how low interest rates are, you're losing money. There's less money than there's ever been in the history of recorded music, so that gives me anxiety. It's weird to say that owning cryptocurrency soothes that anxiety, because it's counterintuitive, but it does."

He is far from the only one hoping cryptocurrency will assuage his financial worries. Internet forums and Twitter accounts devoted to the subject abound with speculators who view digital coins as a lottery ticket, forecasting "moonshots" with, perhaps, irrational exuberance. For office drudges, the underemployed or those crushed by college loans, the slim chance that a $100 investment may someday reap close to $100 million — as would have happened with an investment of that amount in Bitcoin in 2010 — is too enticing to pass up.

But there are plenty of dissenters who are less sanguine about the future of cryptocurrency, arguing that we are in the midst of the biggest bubble yet, fueled by speculative trading in Japan and South Korea, and pointing to previous Bitcoin crashes as justification for their skepticism.

Nevertheless, it's not just twentysomethings in the gig economy who are losing faith in traditional investment tools. Mr. Ginn quit working at Fidelity Investments the day before the market crash in 2008.

"It's not investing," he said of his old job. "It's just sticking money somewhere. The investment advisory industry has to give out watered-down, averaged-out advice. When you get into mutual funds, you lose a lot of the ability to beat the markets."

Tom Berg, 44, a founder of BloKtek Capital in Northbrook, Ill., which invests in digital currencies and assets, said: "I got out of the stock market years ago. My personal opinion was I'm not going to fight for 2 or 3 percent. It's a conservative place." By contrast, digital currencies — his preferred term to cryptocurrency, which he says carries the stigma of black-market money laundering — have disrupted the internet and created a major opportunity for those willing to jump in early, Mr. Berg believes. "At first it was an internet of information," he said. "Then it evolved to an internet of things — social media, I can buy this, I can sell stuff. Now it's the internet of value."

In his view, cryptocurrency left the "dark ages" six months ago, when it was still the domain of "a lot of people who believed in anarchy." He thinks that cryptocurrency is a good five years from going mainstream and that the bubble will burst some time after that, at which point he will sell his assets.

"If my landscaper ever asks me about crypto, that's the day I get out," he said.

There are some barriers to mass popularity. Investors must have enough familiarity with and trust of the internet to send money through a cryptocurrency exchange, such as Coinbase or Poloniex. Some of the exchanges also have elaborate and slow identity-verification processes, and certain states do not permit users to invest on them yet. But it's continually getting easier, and various exchanges allow credit cards for speedy purchases.

Once one has bought digital coins, the threat of hacking remains a serious concern. Even users savvy enough to use two-factor authentication on their phones may not have the know-how to set up "cold storage," or a system of storing coins offline (such as on a computer or dedicated piece of hardware not connected to the internet). There is no Federal Deposit Insurance Corporation insuring lost money; once it's gone, it's gone.

Assuming one's money is protected, there are, of course, the standard risks of investing, amplified by the volatility of cryptocurrency. It's common for a coin to fluctuate double-digit percentages within a day, often because of "pump-and-dump" techniques from coordinated users trying to manipulate prices in completely unregulated free markets.

For this reason, none of the investors I spoke with engage in short-term trading but instead choose, in the online parlance of cryptocurrency enthusiasts, to "hodl" ("hold on for dear life," rather than sell off for temporary gains). Mr. Dinges and his wife recently bought a house in Los Angeles, but he didn't use his Bitcoins to help with the renovations.

"This is a great opportunity to pull it out and put it toward fixing the house," he said, "but the future potential is not worth it."

Mr. Berg would agree, advising BloKtek Capital clients to "set it and forget it" and not fall prey to the temptation to make short-term transactions.

"My wife and I use it as our bank account," he said. "Every paycheck, we put a percentage into long-term holdings. We do not expect to become rich overnight. That's a way to become very poor in one hour." (Though his wife works at his company, it bears mentioning here that the vast majority of cryptocurrency investors seem to be male, and their Twitter discourse tends to be less than refined, with insults often lodged at devotees of rival currencies.)

Even those in it for the long haul, however, admit to monitoring the prices compulsively, scratching the gambler's itch.

"If I have a moment where the price has left my mind, I'll want to reinsert it," Mr. Wax, the record producer, said. "I check it as much as any social media. It's become as distracting as anything else on my phone."

As he works in the cryptocurrency world, Mr. Berg maintains an even more observant — and most likely exhausting — regimen.

"I'm always watching the markets," he said. "The saying is, 'Crypto never sleeps.' It's 24/7, it's global, it doesn't have a stock market, it doesn't have a bell.

"I sleep about four hours a day."

Beyond its potential long-term financial rewards, many holders of cryptocurrency view it as a vehicle for social change. While many coins have no value beyond serving as a potential alternative currency, or began as larks that have since been popularized by speculators (such as Dogecoin, whose logo is an internet-meme dog and which now has a market capitalization of about $200 million), others — namely Ripple and Ethereum — have meaningful real-world utility and are being adopted by banks and financial institutions.

"The financial gain is fun, but it's really about improving the world, improving the financial system, transparency, cost, increased speed," Mr. Ginn said. "It's the double-sided tape for society. When financial markets collapse, the tape rips people apart and you have a system collapse. Finance got away with it in '08; it almost took the world down, and nothing changed." In lieu of more stringent government oversight, he believes that Ripple can help "reduce systemic risk."

That safety-net altruism drives Yoni Saltzman, 24, who designs robotic mechanisms for aerospace and medical applications. Mr. Saltzman has holdings in four different cryptocurrencies and is working with a small team in New York to develop a digital coin it hopes to introduce within a year. "It's not just about making money," he said. "We like the idea of not only changing the world, but saving the world."

This is, of course, the same vaguely idealistic rationale Silicon Valley executives routinely trot out to justify their ventures, not all of which seem especially concerned with the greater good. In the meantime, those who have boarded the crypto-train frequently proselytize to friends and family. Unsurprisingly, they have more luck with their younger peers. Mr. Guarco, the Duke graduate, has persuaded a few friends to take the plunge.

His older relatives, however, unaccustomed to coins that one can't pluck out of a lint-filled pocket, are a harder sell.

"They usually respond, 'Crypto-what?' " he said.

TEDDY WAYNE's most recent novel, "Loner," is out in paperback.

Is There a Cryptocurrency Bubble? Just Ask Doge.

BY KEVIN ROOSE | SEPT. 15, 2017

JACKSON PALMER no longer thinks it's funny to imitate Doge, the internet meme about a Shiba Inu dog whose awe-struck expressions and garbled syntax (e.g. "Wow. So pizza. Much delicious.") made him a viral sensation several years ago.

But if he did, he might channel Doge to offer a few cautionary words for investors who are falling for cryptocurrency start-ups, Silicon Valley's latest moneymaking craze:

Very bubble. Much scam. So avoid.

Mr. Palmer, the creator of Dogecoin, was an early fan of cryptocurrency, a form of encrypted digital money that is traded from person to person. He saw investors talking about Bitcoin, the oldest and best-known cryptocurrency, and wanted to find a way to poke fun at the hype surrounding the emerging technology.

So in 2013, he built his own cryptocurrency, a satirical mash-up that combined Bitcoin with the Doge meme he'd seen on social media. Mr. Palmer hoped to use Dogecoin to show the absurdity of wagering huge sums of money on unstable ventures.

But investors didn't get the joke and bought Dogecoin anyway, bringing its market value as high as $400 million. Along the way, the currency became a magnet for greed and attracted a group of scammers and hackers who defrauded investors, hyped fake products, and left many of the currency's original backers empty-handed.

Today, Mr. Palmer, 30, is one of the loudest voices warning that a similar fate might soon befall the entire cryptocurrency industry.

"What's happening to crypto now is what happened to Dogecoin," Mr. Palmer told me in a recent interview. "I'm worried that this time, it's on a much grander scale."

Already, there are signs of trouble on the horizon. This week, after Chinese authorities announced a crackdown on virtual currencies, the value of Bitcoin briefly tumbled 30 percent before partially recovering. The value of Dogecoin fell more than 50 percent last week. Its market value by midday Friday was about $100 million.

But there remains no bigger mania among tech investors than cryptocurrency, which some see as an eventual replacement for traditional, government-issued money. Even with the recent declines, the price of Bitcoin has more than tripled this year; another cryptocurrency, Ethereum, has gained more than 2,300 percent. The success of these currencies has minted a new class of "crypto-millionaires" and spawned hundreds of other digital currencies, called altcoins. In addition, it has given rise to an entire category of start-ups that take advantage of cryptocurrency's public ledger system, known as the blockchain.

Many cryptocurrency start-ups have raised money through an initial coin offering, or I.C.O., a type of fund-raising campaign in which investors buy into a new venture using Bitcoin or another cryptocurrency and receive virtual "tokens" instead of stock or voting rights in the company. These tokens grant investors access to a product or service that will be built with the money raised in the I.C.O., such as cloud data storage or access to a new social network.

(If you're having trouble picturing it: Imagine that a friend is building a casino and asks you to invest. In exchange, you get chips that can be used at the casino's tables once it's finished. Now imagine that the value of the chips isn't fixed, and will instead fluctuate depending on the popularity of the casino, the number of other gamblers and the regulatory environment for casinos. Oh, and instead of a friend, imagine it's a stranger on the internet who might be using a fake name, who might not actually know how to build a casino, and whom you probably can't sue for fraud if he steals your money and uses it to buy a Porsche instead. That's an I.C.O.)

Despite the obvious risks of these ventures, investor appetite has been ravenous. A group of Bay Area programmers this year used an

I.C.O. to raise $35 million for their project, an anonymous web browser called Brave, in less than 30 seconds. There have been 140 coin offerings in 2017 that have raised a total of $2.1 billion from investors, according to Coinschedule, a website that tracks the activity.

I.C.O. fever has even infected celebrities. This month, the actress Paris Hilton tweeted that she was "looking forward to participating" in the initial coin offering of LydianCoin, a cryptocurrency project associated with the digital advertising company Gravity4. The boxing star Floyd Mayweather and the rapper the Game have also endorsed coin offerings.

Unlike traditional stock offerings, which are carefully supervised and planned months or years in advance, I.C.O.s are largely unregulated in the United States, although that could soon change. The Securities and Exchange Commission warned investors this year about the growing number of coin offerings, saying that "fraudsters often try to use the lure of new and emerging technologies to convince potential victims to invest their money in scams."

Mr. Palmer predicts that while some I.C.O.s may finance the creation of new and exciting enterprises, many will go up in smoke. He sees echoes of the first dot-com boom, when investors poured money into new and risky ventures only to get burned when the market came to its senses.

"People are treating cryptocurrency now like penny stocks," he said. "It's become a securities market."

Other high-profile skeptics have sounded the alarm about a potential crash in the crypto market, including Jamie Dimon, the chief executive of JPMorgan Chase, who last week called Bitcoin a "fraud," and compared the current digital money craze to the 17th-century Dutch tulip bubble. And even true cryptocurrency believers have started to worry that I.C.O. mania won't end well.

"It's a ticking time bomb," Charles Hoskinson, one of the developers of the cryptocurrency Ethereum, told Bloomberg in July.

When Mr. Palmer's interest in digital money began, just four years ago, cryptocurrency was the sole province of math geeks and early adopters.

Jackson Palmer, creator of Dogecoin, in San Francisco in September 2017. He was an early fan of cryptocurrency, but is now one of the loudest voices warning of a crash in the market.

"It was fun, nobody took it seriously," he recalled. "People threw it around like change because it wasn't worth anything."

Unlike Bitcoin, whose early adopters often used it to buy drugs, weapons, or other illicit goods on the dark web, Dogecoin attracted a crowd of earnest do-gooders at first. They even set up a philanthropic arm, called the Dogecoin Foundation, and used it to raise thousands of dollars for projects, including sponsoring service dogs for autistic children and drilling water wells in Kenya. (Their generosity extended to quirkier projects; when Dogecoin fans heard that Jamaica's two-man bobsled team had qualified for the Winter Olympics in Sochi but lacked the money to get to Russia, they pitched in $30,000 to fund the trip.)

As the price of Bitcoin climbed, investors got interested in other cryptocurrencies. With no explanation, the price of Dogecoin doubled, then tripled. Two months after it was introduced, Mr. Palmer's joke was worth $50 million, and some early Dogecoin adopters, who called themselves "shibes," were sitting on lucrative stockpiles.

The success of Dogecoin attracted unsavory characters. One scammer raised $750,000 from Dogecoin supporters for a cryptocurrency start-up that never materialized. A hacker broke into Dogewallet, a website where users stored their coins, and stole thousands of dollars worth of the currency. Soon, the Dogecoin Reddit forum was full of angry scam victims and get-rich-quick schemers, and the once tight-knit Dogecoin community started to disintegrate.

"We tried to do everything right," said Ben Doernberg, a former board member of the Dogecoin Foundation. "But when you have a situation where people stand to put in a dollar and take out a thousand dollars, people lose their minds."

Mr. Palmer, a laid-back Australian who works as a product manager in the Bay Area and describes himself as "socialist leaning," was disturbed by the commercialization of his joke currency. He had never collected Dogecoin for himself, and had resisted efforts to cash in on the currency's success, even turning down a $500,000 investment offer from an Australian venture capital firm.

In 2015, he announced he was leaving Dogecoin behind, telling an interviewer that the cryptocurrency market "increasingly feels like a bunch of white libertarian bros sitting around hoping to get rich and coming up with half-baked, buzzword-filled business ideas."

He recently began making a series of YouTube videos that explain tech topics to beginners, including how digital currencies work. His goal? To rekindle people's excitement in the core blockchain technology, while tamping down some of the excessive hype.

"My mission in all of this is to help people better understand things, rather than just thinking about profit," he said.

It may be too late for that. Regulators in the United States have begun to scrutinize I.C.O.s, and China's central bank went as far as issuing a temporary ban on new coin offerings. But more dollars are still pouring into cryptocurrency ventures every day, as giddy investors ignore the warning signs and look to multiply their money.

Mr. Palmer worries that the coming reckoning in the cryptocurrency market — and it is coming, he says confidently — will deter people from using the technology for more legitimate projects.

"The bigger this bubble goes, the bigger negative connotation it's going to have," he said. "It's going to be like the dot-com bust, but on a much more epic scale."

Everyone Is Getting Hilariously Rich and You're Not

BY NELLIE BOWLES | JAN. 13, 2018

SAN FRANCISCO — Recently the founder of something called Ripple briefly became richer than Mark Zuckerberg. Another day an anonymous donor set up an $86 million Bitcoin-fortune charity called the Pineapple Fund. A Tesla was spotted with a BLOCKHN license plate. There's a surge in people looking to buy Bitcoin on their credit cards. After the Long Island Iced Tea company announced it would pivot to blockchain, its stock rose 500 percent in a day.

In 2017, the cryptocurrency Bitcoin went from $830 to $19,300, and now quivers around $14,000. Ether, its main rival, started the year at less than $10, closing out 2017 at $715. Now it's over $1,100. The wealth is intoxicating news, feverish because it seems so random. Investors trying to grok the landscape compare it to the dot-com bubble of the late 1990s, when valuations soared and it was hard to separate the Amazons and Googles from the Pets.coms and eToys.

The cryptocurrency community is centered around a tightknit group of friends — developers, libertarians, Redditors and cypherpunks — who have known each other for years through meet-ups, an endless circuit of crypto conferences and internet message boards. Over long hours in anonymous group chats, San Francisco bars and Settlers of Catan game nights, they talk about how cryptocurrency will decentralize power and wealth, changing the world order.

The goal may be decentralization, but the money is extremely concentrated. Coinbase has more than 13 million accounts that own cryptocurrencies. Data suggests that about 94 percent of the Bitcoin wealth is held by men, and some estimate that 95 percent of the wealth is held by 4 percent of the owners.

There are only a few winners here, and, unless they lose it all, their impact going forward will be outsize.

Fredric Fortier wears an Ethereum sweater along with Mathiu Baril wearing a Bitcoin sweater at the San Francisco Bitcoin Meetup Holiday Party at the Runway Incubator in December.

They also remember who laughed at them and when.

James Spediacci and his twin brother, Julian, who bought ether when it was about 30 cents, now run one of the most popular whale clubs: private cryptocurrency trading communities where crypto syndicates are coordinated in group chats. He showed me a screen shot of his Facebook post from 2014 telling everyone to buy ether.

"One like," he said, pointing to his phone. "It got one like."

INSIDE THE CRYPTO CASTLE

Whether it's all built on sand or not, the crypto castle has risen. There's an actual house called the Crypto Castle, and the king is Jeremy Gardner, 25, a rakish young investor with a hedge fund who has become the de facto tour guide for crypto newcomers.

Early one afternoon, he opened a bottle of rosé while he charged half a dozen external batteries so he wouldn't have to ever plug in his phone in Ibiza, Spain, the next week.

"I do I.C.O.s. It's my thing," he said. He wore a pink button-front and pink pants. "It's me, a couple V.C.s and a lot of charlatans."

An initial coin offering is a way to raise money: A company creates its own cryptocurrency and investors buy into the new coin, without actually buying a stake in the company. Mr. Gardner led an I.C.O. for his start-up Augur, creating an "Augur token" that he then sold to raise real world money. These tokens sold fast, and it is one of the forces that kicked off this boom. For a time, the value of Augur, a market-forecasting start-up with few customers, exceeded $1 billion.

About eight people live in the Crypto Castle on any given night, and some of Mr. Gardner's tenants brought out snacks (Cheez-Its and a jar of Nutella). One of the bedrooms has a stripper pole. Mr. Gardner leaned back into the sofa and rested his feet on the table. He recently did an I.C.O. for a start-up after-party. "You can I.C.O. anything," he said. He runs Distributed, a 180-page magazine about cryptocurrency that comes out about once a year. He is now raising $75 million for his hedge fund, Ausum Ventures (pronounced "awesome"). He said his closest friends are moving to Puerto Rico to get around paying taxes.

"They're going to build a modern-day Atlantis out there," he said. "But for me, it's too early in my career to check out."

He wears a bracelet from his Burning Man camp (Mayan Warrior) and a necklace that is a key on a chain. "I was given this necklace and was told my net worth would go up, and it's gone up six x since then," he said.

He drew a chart to explain the crypto community: 20 percent for ideology, 60 percent for the tech and 100 percent for the money, he said, drawing a circle around it all.

A roommate on the sofa perked up and asked if he'd ever invest in his lucid dreams start-up (the idea is a headpiece that induces them). Mr. Gardner did not seem impressed: "Probably not," he said. A reality show wants to follow him around, but he's skeptical that it can add to his life.

"I literally have a date with Bella Hadid not having a reality show," he said.

Jeremy Gardner at the Crypto Castle in San Francisco, where he lives.

A few weeks after we first met, as the Bitcoin price exploded in December, Mr. Gardner seemed shaken. People had begun making pilgrimages to the Crypto Castle, knocking on the door, hoping Mr. Gardner could help them invest.

"Nothing feels real, it doesn't feel real," he said. "I'm ready for crypto assets to go down 90 percent. I'll feel better then, I think. This has been too insane."

ENTER THE CRYPTO CRACKHOUSE

Nearby is a building residents call the Crypto Crackhouse.

Grant Hummer, who runs the San Francisco Ethereum Meetup, lives there. Long hallways called Bitcoin Boulevard and Ethereum Alley lead to communal bathrooms. Mr. Hummer and his co-founder committed $40 million of their own crypto-made money to their new $100 million hedge fund, Chromatic Capital.

"My neurons are fried from all the volatility," Mr. Hummer said. "I don't even care at this point. I'm numb to it. I'll lose a million dollars in a day and I'm like, O.K."

His room is simple: a bed, a futon, a TV on a mostly empty media console, three keyboard cleaning sprays and a half dozen canisters of Lysol wipes. His T-shirt reads, "The Lizard of Wall Street," with a picture of a lizard in a suit, dollar-sign necklaces around its neck. He carries with him a coin that reads, "memento mori," to remind himself he can die any day. He sees the boom as part of a global apocalypse.

"The worse regular civilization does and the less you trust, the better crypto does," Mr. Hummer said. "It's almost like the ultimate short trade."

Mr. Hummer went out to meet Joe Buttram, 27, for drinks. As a mixed martial arts fighter, Mr. Buttram said he would fight for a couple hundred bucks, sometimes a few thousand, and worked security at a start-up, but his main hobbies were reading 4chan and buying vintage pornography, passions that exposed him to cryptocurrency.

He said his holdings are into double-digit millions but wouldn't give specifics other than to say he'd quit his job and is starting a hedge fund. There's a common paranoia among the crypto-wealthy that they'll be targeted and robbed since there's no bank securing the money, so many are obsessively secretive. Many say even their parents don't know how much they've made. This also allows people to pretend to be wealthier than they are, of course.

"It's unforgiving," Mr. Buttram said. "You make one mistake and it's all gone."

They talk about buying Lamborghinis, the single acceptable way to spend money in the Ethereum cryptocurrency community. The currency's founder frequently appears in fan art as Jesus with a Lamborghini. Mr. Buttram says he's renting an orange Lambo for the weekend. And he wears a solid gold Bitcoin "B" necklace encrusted with diamonds that he had made. Otherwise, HODL.

This is one of the core beliefs in this community: HODL, "hold" typed very fast, as if in a panic. HODL even if you feel FUD — fear,

James Fickel holding his Russian blue cat, Mr. Bigglesworth, at his apartment in San Francisco.

uncertainty and doubt. If you show wealth, it means you don't really believe in the cryptocurrency revolution, a full remake of the financial system, governments and our world order that will send the price of ether up astronomically.

"HODL when everyone has FUD," Mr. Hummer said quietly, to explain why he still lives in a dorm room. "This will change civilization. This can 100 x or more from here."

He knows this is strange.

"When I meet people in the normal world now, I get bored," Mr. Hummer said. "It's just a different level of consciousness."

The tone turns somber. "Sometimes I think about what would happen to the future if a bomb went off at one of our meetings," Mr. Buttram said.

Mr. Hummer said, "A bomb would set back civilization for years."

A few days later, Mr. Hummer was working from his co-founder's apartment.

James Fickel, 26, lives in a high-rise with a Russian blue cat called Mr. Bigglesworth. Mr. Fickel is known in the community for "going full YOLO" and investing $400,000 when Ethereum was at 80 cents. Now, with a fortune he says is in the hundreds of millions, his parents have retired and sent his younger sister to live with him.

"I'm taking over her education," Mr. Fickel said, sitting on a white leather sofa, Mr. Bigglesworth asleep in his impossibly skinny arms.

Today, Mr. Fickel is outlining the endgame for cryptocurrency true believers.

"It's the entire world reorganizing itself," Mr. Fickel said. "We could get rid of our armies because for the first time you'll have people saying, 'I want to vote for a global order.' It's the internet waking up — it's the internet grabbing its pitchfork. That's the blockchain."

Mr. Hummer is skeptical.

"All I know is the price of ether is going to go up," Mr. Hummer said.

At a jazz bar a few days later, I run into Mr. Fickel's personal trainer, Alan Chen, who is now running in this crypto circle. Mr. Fickel had convinced Mr. Chen to put his savings into Ethereum.

"I'm retired, man," Mr. Chen said. "I'm moving to L.A. next week. I got a penthouse on Marina del Rey."

"Don't say I'm retired," he added. "I'm going into business now. I'm going to use blockchain to help personal trainers."

Nearby was Chante Eliaszadeh, 22, a law student at the University of California, Berkeley, who started the Berkeley Law Blockchain group.

"Obviously the bubble's going to burst and everyone's going to need a lawyer," she said.

THE BITCOIN MEETUP GROUP THROWS A PARTY

At the annual San Francisco Bitcoin Meetup Party, hundreds gathered under the fluorescent lights of a co-working space, and there was a line out the door. The waiting list had to be told not to show up. Many there wore Bitcoin- and Ethereum-themed clothes from Hodlmoon, which sells unisex cryptocurrency sweaters.

Those closest to the technology are the most cautious. Pieter Wuille, 33, a Bitcoin core developer, kept his backpack on as he wandered the party. He's part of the team working to develop the Bitcoin technology.

"The technology still needs time to evolve," Mr. Wuille said. "This infusion of interest is bringing the wrong kind of attention. Some people believe Bitcoin can't fail or this technology solves many more problems than it does. It can. And it does not."

He said everyone is asking him whether to buy Bitcoin. "I tell them I have no idea," he said. "I don't know!"

"There's so many people rushing into the space, if it's a bit of speculation, I'm O.K. with that," said the Coinbase C.E.O., Brian Armstrong, whose company has become the de facto portal for casual investors. "But we can't guarantee the website's going to be up exactly when you need it. Everyone needs to take a deep breath."

As the holiday party filled up, a cryptocurrency rapper called Coin-Daddy — Arya Bahmanyar, 28 — was getting ready to perform.

JASON HENRY FOR THE NEW YORK TIMES

Arya Bahmanyar, 28, also known as "Coin Daddy," at the San Francisco Bitcoin Meetup Holiday Party at the Runway Incubator in San Francisco.

Formerly a commercial real estate agent, Mr. Bahmanyar works full time at CoinDaddy after becoming a self-described crypto-millionaire ("you think I would dress up like this if I wasn't?"). "Right now all our entertainers come from outside crypto culture — not inside crypto, and we've got to change that," he said.

He pointed to his outfit — a long white fake mink coat, gold-heeled shoes — and said, "It's gold, right? It's gold. It's a niche, and I'm going to fill it."

He says he is going to shoot a music video soon for a song called "Lambo Party" and another called "Cryptomom," about "all these moms are pumping in their children's savings accounts."

Maria Lomeli, 56, came to the party to find the people she had put a lot of trust in. A housekeeper from Pacifica, Calif., she said she had invested $12,000 in cryptocurrencies over the last few weeks after reading about it in the news.

She wore running shoes and a zip-up jacket that said, "Cinemark, the best seats in town." She worked there cleaning out theaters. Now she cleans houses. Banks, she said, were designed to steal. Taxes left her supporting a government that she felt didn't support her.

"Charges for sending money to my daughter, interest on our loans," she said. "And then the money we pay in taxes goes to wars and whatever else they want."

She found a Bitcoin event in the city and asked people there how to buy Bitcoin on her phone. She invested $1,000. It went up. So she put in $10,000 more, she said, along with $1,000 in a currency called Litecoin. Both her children have discouraged this.

"And maybe I'm going to lose it," she said. "Maybe I'm going to keep cleaning houses. But something is telling me I can trust this generation. My instinct is telling me this is the future."

She had to leave the party early because parking downtown is expensive, she said. She zipped up her jacket and left on her own.

Bitcoin Falls Below $10,000 as Virtual Currency Bubble Deflates

BY NATHANIEL POPPER AND NELLIE BOWLES | JAN. 17, 2018

SAN FRANCISCO — The air has been swiftly leaking out of the virtual currency bubble.

A decline in virtual currency prices that began before Christmas has picked up pace in recent days as concern has grown that governments could crack down on the new industry.

For a time on Wednesday, the price of Bitcoin dipped below $10,000 — taking it down to about half what it was at its peak last month.

Other virtual currencies have been falling even faster. Ripple, which was briefly second in value after Bitcoin, has lost more than two-thirds of its value from the high it hit early this month.

The falling prices have been serious enough to prompt online posts with suicide hotlines for virtual currency investors in despair.

The declines are likely to be particularly painful for people who took out debt to buy virtual currencies at high prices. Even the lows hit on Wednesday are still well up — some 1,000 percent — from where Bitcoin began 2017. But that is little comfort for the people who purchased late last year.

One person on Reddit wrote about persuading family members to buy digital tokens late in 2017 and regretting it.

"Fast forward to today," the user, going by the screen name PM_ME_UR_ROOM_VIEW, wrote. "I opened my phone and I find a barrage of messages from them accusing me of scamming them and tricking them into crypto because they lost money, I tried to explain to them that this is normal and it will bounce back soon and it's just a correction and don't sell but they aren't listening."

For skeptics of virtual currencies, the falling prices have provided some vindication.

"Most people are buying Bitcoin, not because of a belief in its future as a global currency, but because they expect it to rise in value," a note from economists at Capital Economics said on Wednesday. "Accordingly, it has all the hallmarks of a classic speculative bubble, which we expect to burst."

The pessimism in recent days has been fed by several reports that governments around the world were planning to tighten the reins on virtual currency trading.

South Korean officials have said they were contemplating shutting down the virtual currency exchanges that have popped up over the past year. South Korea has seen the most frenzied surge of ordinary investors throwing their savings into Bitcoin and other digital tokens.

The Chinese government has already shut down exchanges in China, but it was recently reported to be taking even further measures against new forms of online trading as well as Bitcoin mining operations in the country.

Regulators in the United States have continued to crack down on smaller virtual currencies like Bitconnect, which has been described as a Ponzi scheme by many in the industry.

Bitcoin, which began in 2009, has been through these sorts of wild swings before. The price spiked in late 2013 to above $1,000, before moves by the Chinese government sent the price sliding. It was only last year that the price again recovered to the same levels.

Since that recovery, an array of virtual currencies have been on a nearly uninterrupted tear. With Bitcoin, investors have been betting that it could be a new kind of asset, outside the control of any government, something like digital gold.

Investors have also been putting money into newer virtual currencies like Ethereum and Ripple, which were designed to do more sophisticated types of transactions than Bitcoin.

The excitement has been amplified by hedge funds that were created in the last year to invest in virtual currencies and by Wall Street institutions that have expressed an interest.

But investments in these new tokens have far outstripped their real-world use in the types of transactions for which they are intended. Ripple, for example, is supposed to help financial institutions transfer money across international borders. But only a few institutions have said they are using the currency, known as XRP, for that purpose.

Some longtime virtual currency investors have said that a major price pullback was necessary after the hype had gotten so far ahead of the reality.

"This is the ecosystem purging the 'easy money' crowd that arrived in past couple months," Spencer Bogart, a partner with the hedge fund Blockchain Capital, wrote on Twitter.

Prominent individual investors echoed that sentiment. "I usually recommend people to buy during dips like these if they were hesitant to enter the market before because you can get in on a discount," said James Spediacci, who with his brother Julian runs an investment club for virtual currency investors.

Monica Quaintance, lead engineer at a company working on technology related to digital currencies and an organizer of events for women interested in them, said investors should expect price volatility until there is strong government regulation. "People want to know that if they make a lot of money from Bitcoin they're going to be able to keep the money," Ms. Quaintance said.

But for those less enamored of the technology, the declines are viewed as the beginning of an even steeper fall.

"The latest price falls suggest that the bubble is bursting — although with prices still ten times higher than a year ago, they have a lot further to fall yet," Capital Economics wrote.

CHAPTER 4

Mainstreaming Bitcoin: Inventing Business Models

Though Bitcoin and other currencies began in communities, the profit potential turned virtual money into big business. Financial institutions explored cryptocurrencies for their possible security. Investors such as the Winklevoss twins became Bitcoin billionaires, and exchanges such as Coinbase became cryptocurrencies' equivalent to Nasdaq. Crucially, the task of generating new coins shifted from individual computers to cryptocurrency "mines," which pool processing power to generate millions of dollars at enormous energy costs.

Bitcoin Pursues the Mainstream

BY NICK WINGFIELD | OCT. 30, 2013

THE CURRENCY known as Bitcoin — a much-hyped and much-doubted type of digital cash that can be bought with traditional money — has mostly attracted attention for its popularity in the black market, and for its wildly gyrating valuation.

But some entrepreneurs, investors and even merchants are eyeing a far more mainstream use for it. They are convinced that Bitcoin, though not widely understood, offers a path to lower payment processing and more secure transactions. Instead of using Bitcoin to buy illegal guns in the recesses of the web, they say, ordinary consumers will use it to buy legal goods from legal retailers — and as easily as they now swipe their credit cards or exchange paper bills.

"I'm confident you will see major worldwide retailers adopting systems built on Bitcoin," said Jim Breyer, the Silicon Valley venture capitalist and early Facebook investor who also served on the board of Walmart Stores for more than a decade.

Mr. Breyer is an investor in Circle Internet Financial, one of the host of start-ups trying to find a way to make Bitcoin a widely adopted currency for retail payments. The company was started by Jeremy Allaire, a serial entrepreneur, and it aims to be a payment processing system for online and physical merchants, similar to the service PayPal offers online. Along with his venture firm, Accel Partners, and another called General Catalyst Partners, Mr. Breyer has invested $9 million in the company.

One potential obstacle to mainstream acceptance of Bitcoin is the sometimes wild fluctuations in its value, which makes it alluring to currency speculators but could scare off ordinary consumers. One Bitcoin was worth just over $200 Wednesday afternoon. Someone who bought a Bitcoin in early April paid as much as $266 for it.

Only a small and motley assortment of merchants now accept Bitcoin as payment, and in many cases they do it largely as a marketing strategy. The list includes a winery in British Columbia, the popular online dating site OkCupid and a Seattle lunch truck that specializes in grilled cheese sandwiches. A start-up called Gyft lets people buy electronic gift cards for major retailers with Bitcoin, and this week an A.T.M. in Vancouver, Canada, began issuing Bitcoin to people in exchange for cash.

"We pride ourselves on being the nerdiest online dating site," said Sam Yagan, co-founder of OkCupid, which is owned by IAC/InterActiveCorp, a media and Internet company. "We were like, 'This is cool and we should do it.' "

Since Bitcoin emerged in 2009, many of those who flocked to the currency celebrated it for being beyond the clutches of governments

Jeremy Allaire of Circle Internet Financial, which promotes Bitcoin for retail use.

and other institutions. Until recently, the currency lubricated transactions on Silk Road, one of the Web's biggest bazaars for drugs, forged documents and other contraband. The site was shut down in early October by federal authorities.

New Bitcoin is created on computers connected through a peer-to-peer network. An algorithm controls the production of new Bitcoin, which is meant to mitigate the risk of inflation.

Already, though, businesses transferring and exchanging Bitcoin find themselves in regulators' cross hairs.

In March, the Financial Crimes Enforcement Network, part of the Treasury Department, issued guidelines telling businesses involved in the exchange of digital currencies that they needed to register as money services businesses and comply with a variety of rules to prevent money laundering. New York's Department of Financial services began an inquiry in August to determine guidelines for digital currency businesses, issuing nearly two dozen subpoenas to start-ups, investors and others involved in the emerging field.

Patrick M. Byrne, chief executive of the online retailer Overstock .com, said his company was talking about accepting Bitcoin, but it decided to pause its plans until legal matters around the currency were clarified.

Fred Ehrsam, co-founder of Coinbase, a start-up that helps merchants accept Bitcoin and helps consumers obtain it by exchanging traditional currencies, said he thought the demise of Silk Road gave entrepreneurs and investors more confidence in Bitcoin.

"The bad guys basically lost," said Mr. Ehrsam, whose start-up has raised over $6 million from Union Square Ventures and others. "It took the single most illegitimate player in the space and wiped them off the map."

Bitcoin advocates, and especially merchants, say one of the currency's most enticing promises is that it could significantly lower payment processing costs.

Retailers typically pay 2 to 3 percent of the value of a customer sale when a credit card is used. Retailers have long complained about these fees and have sought other options, but without much luck. Pay-Pal, the online payment system, typically charges merchants a fee between 2.2 percent and 2.9 percent, as well as a per-transaction fee of 30 cents.

"There have been a number of alternative currencies talked about over time," said Chris Monteiro, a spokesman for MasterCard. "The bottom line is consumers want a payment solution that is safe, simple to use and universally accepted."

Fees for a merchant accepting Bitcoin payments often range from nothing to less than 2 percent because of the open nature of the technology. Coinbase, for example, said it did not charge its merchants for the first $1 million in sales, imposing a 1 percent fee after that on the conversion of Bitcoin into local currency. Circle said it had not settled on pricing for merchants, but that it would charge them a fee to use its system that would be well below credit card transaction costs.

Mr. Allaire and others predict that merchants will encourage customers to spend Bitcoin by passing some of the savings on to them in the form of lower prices or other rewards.

"Bitcoin definitely addresses a need," said Simon Johnson, a professor at the M.I.T. Sloan School of Management. "The payments industry is ready to be disrupted."

The fluctuating value of Bitcoin has not stopped some investors. Tyler and Cameron Winklevoss, the twin brothers who tangled with Mark Zuckerberg over the founding of Facebook, have said they are big holders of Bitcoin and have filed a proposal with securities regulators that would let investors trade Bitcoin as if it were stocks.

Other challenges face Circle and other start-ups building new payment systems. For example, it can take several business days to link someone's bank account to their Bitcoin. Mr. Allaire of Circle said one of his goals was to make that initial setup much faster.

Mr. Allaire also said his company, which is based in Boston, will protect its customers' Bitcoin by creating "offline reserves" — batches of the digital currency on physical storage devices, like a hard drive, not connected to the Internet. The offline Bitcoin reserves will be protected by armed guards, he said.

George Peabody, senior director at Glenbrook Partners, a consultancy in the payments industry, said Circle was a sign of the maturation of entrepreneurs entering the Bitcoin market.

Mr. Allaire was an early web entrepreneur, founding a web application development company, Allaire Corporation, that went public in 1999 and was sold to Macromedia. An Internet video company he created, Brightcove, went public last year. Mr. Allaire said he was convinced that Bitcoin represented another major technological development.

"It's similar to me in import as the web browser," he said. "It's as exciting and significant as that."

Data Security Is Becoming the Sparkle in Bitcoin

BY SYDNEY EMBER | MARCH 1, 2015

SOME COUPLES OPT for a traditional wedding, while others go for the Elvis impersonator in Las Vegas. But David Mondrus and Joyce Bayo may be the first to have incorporated Bitcoin.

Before about 50 guests at a Walt Disney World hotel in Florida recently, the couple used a Bitcoin automated teller machine to record their written vows on the currency's so-called block chain — an open ledger that permanently stores information.

"A diamond is forever, a marriage is forever, but when was the last time anyone looked at their wedding vows?" Mr. Mondrus said. "This technology allows us to get that data and store it in a way that is retrievable and noncorruptible."

As Bitcoin's price has declined over the last year, critics have been quick to declare the virtual currency dead. Bitcoin's true value, though, might be not in the currency itself but in the engine that makes it possible.

Underlying Bitcoin — created as a way to make payments directly, anonymously and outside government control — is the block chain, a decentralized database that is driven by cryptography.

Explaining how the block chain works can tangle the tongues of even those who are most enthusiastic about Bitcoin. Most resort to metaphors or diagrams. At a basic level, the block chain is a searchable ledger where all transactions are confirmed, in a matter of minutes, by a network of computers working to perform complex algorithms. Each part of the network maintains a copy of the ledger. About six times an hour, a new group of accepted transactions — a block — is created, added to the chain and broadcast to the other parts of the network. In this manner, all transactions are recorded and linked and thus can be traced. It is nearly impossible to modify past blocks in the chain.

By simply downloading the Bitcoin software, anyone can gain access to the block chain, search it and submit transactions to the network.

Entrepreneurs worldwide are now working to harness that technology for use beyond Bitcoin transactions. The block chain, they say, could ultimately upend not only the traditional financial system but also the way people transfer and record financial assets like stocks, contracts, property titles, patents and marriage licenses — essentially anything that requires a trusted middleman for verification.

"There's a race going on to extend the block chain's capabilities," said Adam Ludwin, a co-founder of Chain.com, a start-up that seeks to help developers build Bitcoin applications.

On web forums and at Bitcoin conferences, talk is shifting to the next generation of applications built on block-chain technology. So-called Bitcoin 2.0 projects dominated the conversation at the Satoshi Roundtable, a retreat for Bitcoin enthusiasts at a resort in the Dominican Republic in February, according to accounts from some participants. About 20 percent of Chain's roughly 5,000 users are developing nonfinancial block-chain applications, compared with less than 10 percent a year ago, Mr. Ludwin said. Banks and multinational telecommunications companies are quietly expressing interest in ways to take advantage of the block chain.

Investors are also starting to bet on the technology. Through the end of February, Bitcoin companies had raised $550 million in venture capital, according to Wedbush Securities, a financial services firm. And although much of that financing has been directed to trading platforms, exchanges and digital-wallet start-ups — $106 million alone has gone to Coinbase, a popular provider of Bitcoin wallets — companies working on block-chain applications are beginning to secure chunks of financing.

For instance, Blockstream — which is looking to extend the block chain's capabilities — announced it had raised $21 million in November. Ripple Labs, which oversees an online payment system called Ripple, has raised $9 million and is finalizing another round of financing.

The offices of Chain.com, a start-up that helps developers build Bitcoin applications.

Among the venture capital firms that have backed Bitcoin-related companies is Khosla Ventures, an investor in Blockstream and Chain. Keith Rabois, a partner at Khosla, said the firm's investments were based on the conviction that the block chain would alter the way society thought about transactions — financial or otherwise.

"Anytime there's a broker — anytime there's an expert attesting to the validity of something — all of that could be obviated by the block chain," Mr. Rabois said. "It's not a guaranteed success, but the upside is so large that as a venture investor, it's an extremely attractive investment opportunity."

Several start-ups are developing ways to transfer traditional money using the block chain in the hopes of streamlining financial transactions. One such company, Coins.ph, based in the Philippines, has seized on the block chain's peer-to-peer technology as a way to improve the remittance business and global payments by lowering costs and speeding up transactions. The company's goal is for people to use its services without having to understand the block chain, much as people send email without thinking about the Internet.

"The way I think of the block chain is a really modern infrastructure to move money around the globe," said Marwan Forzley, the chief executive of Align Commerce, another start-up seeking to make cross-border payments easier.

Although companies focused on financial applications for the block chain far outnumber those experimenting with other uses, the gap is narrowing. For example, a start-up called BlockSign verifies signed documents on the block chain. Another company, Filecoin, is aiming to build a marketplace for storing data on the block chain.

PeerNova — which said it was planning to announce financing that would bring its total to about $20 million — is developing a technology that will use the block chain to prove the authenticity of a document, like a patent. The company is also toying with registry applications for other records, including title deeds and financial data.

"Our entire system of contracts is based on a trusted third party," said Naveed Sherwani, the chief executive of PeerNova. But with the block chain, he added, "there is no third party anymore."

With the rise of the block chain has come a fundamental question: Should technology replace human discretion? Some experts, even those who study cryptocurrency, are skeptical.

"There are very good reasons why we have legal and social institutions and economic intermediaries," said Arvind Narayanan, an assistant professor of computer science at Princeton who studies block-chain technology.

In his teaching, Professor Narayanan said he often used car ownership as an example. In theory, block-chain technology could eliminate the need for, among other inconveniences, title certificates and dealers to ensure the secure transfer of money and property. The idea initially sounds appealing, but if the car is broken into or stolen, he said, the block chain alone will not be able to resolve the dispute.

"It's not just one human you're getting rid of, but the entire economic, legal and social structure that reinforces the idea of property," he said.

There is also still broad support for Bitcoin. Many investors and entrepreneurs maintain that Bitcoin will outgrow its early role as a speculative investment and become a viable alternative currency for international payments. Others see countries turning to Bitcoin when their own currency is unstable.

The virtual currency must also maintain some value for the network to work. Bitcoin miners, the computers that drive the block chain, win bitcoins if they successfully solve complex cryptographic problems. If Bitcoin's value continues to drop, it could become too expensive to keep the computers running.

But there are also those wary of moving too fast. Though enthusiastic about the block chain's potential, a group of Bitcoin supporters, many of them early adopters, wants start-ups to focus first on strengthening existing Bitcoin applications, like digital wallets and trading platforms, before developing other uses for the underlying technology.

Exchanges, where traders can meet to buy and sell bitcoins for dollars, euros and other currencies, have been especially vulnerable. Anxiety from the collapse last year of Mt. Gox, a prominent exchange based in Japan, is still high. And a security breach in January at Bitstamp, another exchange, sent further ripples of doubt through the Bitcoin industry.

"People are rightfully talking about the block chain," said Jeremy Liew, a partner at Lightspeed Venture Partners, a venture capital firm that has invested in a number of Bitcoin start-ups, including Blockchain, a digital-wallet provider and software developer, and BTCChina, a Chinese exchange. "The question is how do you realize the first opportunity here?"

"You can't jump to the top of the stairs," he added. "Everything is a process."

How China Took Center Stage in Bitcoin's Civil War

BY NATHANIEL POPPER | JUNE 29, 2016

A DELEGATION of American executives flew to Beijing in April for a secret meeting at the Grand Hyatt hotel, just blocks from Tiananmen Square. They went to meet with the new kingmakers in what has become one of the grandest and strangest experiments in money the world has seen: the virtual currency known as Bitcoin.

Against long odds, and despite an abstruse structure, in which super-computers are said to mine the currency via mathematical formulas, Bitcoin has become a multibillion-dollar industry. It has attracted major investments from Silicon Valley and a significant following on Wall Street.

Yet Bitcoin, which is both a new kind of digital money and an unusual financial network, is having something of an identity crisis. Like so many technologies before it, the virtual currency is coming up against the inevitable push and pull between commercial growth and the purity of its original ambitions.

In its early conception, Bitcoin was to exist beyond the control of any single government or country. It would be based everywhere and nowhere.

Yet despite the talk of a borderless currency, a handful of Chinese companies have effectively assumed majority control of the Bitcoin network. They have done so through canny investments and vast farms of computer servers dispersed around the country. The American delegation flew to Beijing because that was where much of the Bitcoin power was concentrated.

At the time of the meeting, over 70 percent of the transactions on the Bitcoin network were going through just four Chinese companies, known as Bitcoin mining pools — and most flowed through just two of those companies. That gives them what amounts to veto power over any changes to the Bitcoin software and technology.

China has become a market for Bitcoin unlike anything in the West, fueling huge investments in server farms as well as enormous speculative trading on Chinese Bitcoin exchanges. Chinese exchanges have accounted for 42 percent of all Bitcoin transactions this year, according to an analysis performed for The New York Times by Chainalysis. Just last week, the Chinese internet giant, Baidu, joined with three Chinese banks to invest in the American Bitcoin company Circle.

But China's clout is raising worries about Bitcoin's independence and decentralization, which was supposed to give the technology freedom from the sort of government crackdowns and interventions that are commonplace in the Chinese financial world.

"The concentration in a single jurisdiction does not bode well," said Emin Gun Sirer, a professor at Cornell and a Bitcoin researcher. "We need to pay attention to these things if we want decentralization to be a meaningful thing."

The power of Chinese companies has already come to play a major role in a civil war that has divided Bitcoin followers over the last year and led to the departure of one of the top developers of the virtual currency. The dispute has hinged on technical matters but also on bigger questions of what Bitcoin should look like in 10 or 20 years.

NETWORK BOTTLENECK

The American companies that journeyed to the Grand Hyatt — including venture capital-funded start-ups like Coinbase and Circle — are fighting to make Bitcoin bigger. They hope to expand the capacity of the Bitcoin network so that it can process more transactions and compete with the PayPals and Visas of the world.

The current size of the network goes back to the early days, when Bitcoin's founder, Satoshi Nakamoto, limited the amount of data that could travel through the network, essentially capping it at about seven transactions a second. As Bitcoin has grown more popular, those limits have caused severe congestion and led to lengthy transaction delays.

Bitcoin flows, Jan. 1 through June 1, 2016

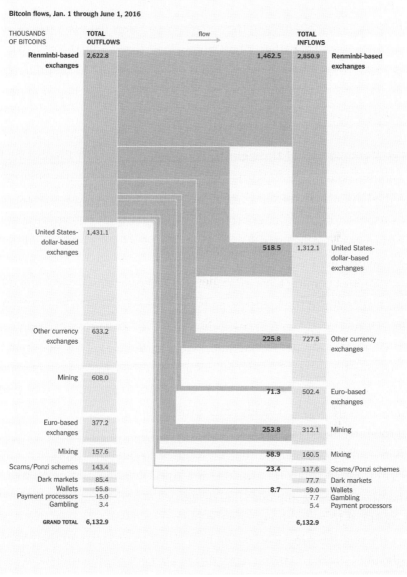

THOUSANDS OF BITCOINS	TOTAL OUTFLOWS		flow →		TOTAL INFLOWS	
Renminbi-based exchanges	2,622.8		1,462.5	2,850.9	Renminbi-based exchanges	
United States-dollar-based exchanges	1,431.1		518.5	1,312.1	United States-dollar-based exchanges	
Other currency exchanges	633.2		225.8	727.5	Other currency exchanges	
Mining	608.0		71.3	502.4	Euro-based exchanges	
Euro-based exchanges	377.2		253.8	312.1	Mining	
Mixing	157.6		58.9	160.5	Mixing	
Scams/Ponzi schemes	143.4		23.4	117.6	Scams/Ponzi schemes	
Dark markets	85.4			77.7	Dark markets	
Wallets	55.8		8.7	59.0	Wallets	
Payment processors	15.0			7.7	Gambling	
Gambling	3.4			5.4	Payment processors	
GRAND TOTAL	6,132.9			6,132.9		

Data on Bitcoin's use reveals that most of the transactions come from exchanges — most of all, exchanges in China — where people speculate on the value of the currency. People using Bitcoin to buy or sell products or services are a fraction of all transactions.

The American delegation in China had a software proposal, known as Bitcoin Classic, that would change all that.

The Chinese companies, though, had the ultimate decision-making power over any changes in the software, and they did not agree with the American delegation. The Chinese had thrown in their lot with another group of longtime programmers who wanted to keep Bitcoin smaller, in part to keep it more secure. The Americans hoped to persuade the Chinese to switch sides.

In a hotel conference room, the American team of about a half-dozen people cycled through its PowerPoint slides, in English and Chinese, arguing for expansion of the network, most notably pointing to the long delays that have been plaguing the system as a result of the congestion. The Chinese companies listened and conferred among themselves. The group took a break for a lunch of lamb and dumplings at a nearby mall.

"We kept coming back and saying, 'For better or worse, you have this leadership in the industry, and everyone is looking to you to show some leadership,' " said Brian Armstrong, chief executive of Coinbase.

Ultimately, Mr. Armstrong said, "We were unable to convince them."

Some Bitcoin advocates have complained that the Chinese companies have been motivated only by short-term profit, rather than the long-term success and ideals of the project. Bobby Lee, chief executive of the Bitcoin company BTCC, which is based in Shanghai, bristled at that — and at the notion that the Chinese companies represent any sort of united front. He attended the April meeting and pointed out that the Chinese companies had disagreed among themselves on how urgent it is to make changes to the Bitcoin software.

He said the American companies failed to understand the power dynamics in the room that day. "It was almost like imperialistic Westerners coming to China and telling us what to do," Mr. Lee said in an interview last week. "There has been a history on this. The Chinese people have long memories."

A MINING POWERHOUSE

The mysterious creator of Bitcoin, Satoshi Nakamoto, released the software in early 2009. It was designed to provide both a digital coin and a new way to move and hold money, much as email had made it possible to send messages without using a postal service.

From the beginning, the system was designed to be decentralized — operated by all the people who joined their computers to the Bitcoin network and helped to process the transactions, as Wikipedia entries are written and maintained by volunteers around the world.

The appeal of a group-run network was that there would be no single point of failure and no company that could shut things down if the police intervened. This was censorship-free money, Bitcoin followers liked to say. Decision-making power for the network resided with the people who joined it, in proportion to the computing power they provided.

The allure of new riches provided the incentive to join: Every 10 minutes, new bitcoins would be released and given to one of the computers helping to maintain the system. In the lingo of Bitcoin, these computers were said to be "mining" for currency. They also served as accountants for the network.

For the first few years, aside from its use as a payment method on the Silk Road, an online drug market that has since been shut down, Bitcoin failed to gain much traction. It burst into the world's consciousness in 2013 when the price of the digital money began to spike, in no small part because Chinese investors began trading bitcoins in large numbers.

Mr. Lee said the Chinese took quickly to Bitcoin for several reasons. For one thing, the Chinese government had strictly limited other potential investment avenues, giving citizens a hunger for new assets. Also, Mr. Lee said, the Chinese loved the volatile price of Bitcoin, which gave the fledgling currency network the feeling of online gambling, a very popular activity in China.

There has been widespread speculation that Chinese people have used Bitcoin to get money out of the country and evade capital controls, but Mr. Lee and other experts said the evidence suggests this is not a significant phenomenon.

"No Chinese person is pushing for Bitcoin because it's libertarian or because it's going to cause the downfall of governments," said Mr. Lee, who moved to China after growing up in Africa and the United States and studying at Stanford. "This was an investment."

The extent of the speculative activity in China in late 2013 pushed the price of a single Bitcoin above $1,000. That surge — and the accompanying media spotlight — led China's government to intervene in December 2013 and cut off the flow of money between Chinese banks and Bitcoin exchanges, popping what appeared to be a Bitcoin bubble.

The frenzy, though, awakened interest in another aspect of the currency: Bitcoin mining.

Peter Ng, a former investment manager, is one of the many people in China who moved from trading bitcoins to amassing computing power to mine them. First, he mined for himself. More recently he has created data centers across China where other people can pay to set up their own mining computers. He now has 28 such centers, all of them filled with endless racks of servers, tangled cords and fans cooling the machines.

Mr. Ng, 36, said he had become an expert in finding cheap energy, often in places where a coal plant or hydroelectric dam was built to support some industrial project that never happened. The Bitcoin mining machines in his facilities use about 38 megawatts of electricity, he said, enough to power a small city.

The people who put their machines in Mr. Ng's data centers generally join mining pools, which smooth the financial returns of smaller players. A popular one, BTCC Pool, is run by Mr. Lee's company. This month it attracted about 13 percent of the total computational power on the Bitcoin network. The most powerful pool in China — or anywhere in the world — is known as F2Pool, and it had 27 percent of the network's computational power this month.

THE POLITICS OF POOLS

Big pool operators have become the kingmakers in the Bitcoin world: Running the pools confers the right to vote on changes to Bitcoin's software, and the bigger the pool, the more voting power. If members of a pool disagree, they can switch to another pool. But most miners choose a pool based on its payout structure, not its Bitcoin politics.

It was his role overseeing BTCC Pool that got Mr. Lee invited to the meeting with the American delegation in Beijing. The head of operations at F2Pool, Wang Chun, was also there.

Perhaps the most important player in the Chinese Bitcoin world is Jihan Wu, 30, a former investment analyst who founded what is often described in China as the world's most valuable Bitcoin company. That company, Bitmain, began to build computers in 2013 using chips specially designed to do mining computations.

Bitmain, which now has 250 employees, manufactures and sells Bitcoin mining computers, operates a pool that other miners can join, called Antpool, and also keeps a significant number of mining machines for itself, which it maintains in Iceland and the United States, as well as in China. The machines that Bitmain retains for itself account for 10 percent of the computing power on the global Bitcoin network and are enough to produce new coins worth about $230,000 each day, at the exchange rate this week.

Mr. Wu and the other mining pool operators in China have often seemed somewhat surprised, and even unhappy, that their investments have given them decision-making power within the Bitcoin network. "Miners are the hardware guys. Why are you asking us about software?" is the line that Mr. Ng said he often hears from miners.

This attitude initially led most Chinese miners to align themselves with old-line Bitcoin coders, known as the core programmers, who have resisted changing the software. The miners wanted to take no risks with the money they were minting.

But lately, Mr. Wu has grown increasingly vocal in his belief that the network is going to have to expand, and soon, if it wants to keep its followers. He said in an email this week that if the core programmers did not increase the number of transactions going through the network by July, he would begin looking for alternatives to expand the network.

However the software debate goes, there are fears that China's government could decide, at some point, to pressure miners in the country to use their influence to alter the rules of the Bitcoin network. The government's intervention in 2013 suggests that Bitcoin is not too small to escape notice.

Mr. Wu dismissed that concern. He also said that as more Americans buy his Bitmain machines and take advantage of cheap power in places like Washington State, mining will naturally become more decentralized. Already, he said, 30 to 40 percent of new Bitmain machines are being shipped out of China.

For now, though, China remains dominant.

"The Chinese government normally expects its businesses to obtain a leading role in emerging industries," he said. "China's Bitcoin businesses have achieved that."

DAVID KESTENBAUM and **PAUL MOZUR** contributed reporting.

In China's Hinterlands, Workers Mine Bitcoin for a Digital Fortune

BY CAO LI AND GIULIA MARCHI | SEPT. 13, 2017

DALAD BANNER, CHINA — They worked as factory hands, in the coal business and as farmers. Their spirits rose when a coal boom promised to bring factories and jobs to this land of grassy plains in Inner Mongolia. When the boom ebbed, they looked for work wherever they could.

Today, many have found it at a place that makes money — the digital kind.

Here, in what is locally called the Dalad Economic Development Zone, lies one of the biggest Bitcoin farms in the world. These eight factory buildings with blue-tin roofs account for nearly one-twentieth of the world's daily production of the cryptocurrency.

Based on today's prices, it issues $318,000 in digital currency a day.

GIULIA MARCHI FOR THE NEW YORK TIMES

A Bitmain employee at work at the farm.

From the outside, the factory — owned by a company called Bitmain China — does not look much different from the other buildings in the industrial park.

Its neighbors include chemical plants and aluminum smelters. Some of the buildings in the zone were never finished. Except for the occasional coal-carrying truck, the roads are largely silent.

Inside, instead of heavy industrial machinery, workers tend rows and rows of computers — nearly 25,000 computers in all — crunching the mathematical problems that create Bitcoin.

Workers carry laptop computers as they walk the aisles looking for breakdowns and checking cable connections. They fill water tanks that keep the computers from melting down or bursting into flame. Around them, hundreds of thousands of cooling fans fill the building with whooshing white noise.

Bitcoin's believers say it will be the currency of the future. Purely electronic, it can be sent across borders anonymously without oversight by a central authority. That makes it appealing to a diverse and sometimes mismatched group that includes tech enthusiasts, civil libertarians, hackers and criminals.

Bitcoin is also, by and large, made in China. The country makes more than two-thirds of all Bitcoin issued daily. Bitmain, founded by Jihan Wu, a former investment analyst, makes money mostly by selling equipment to make bitcoins, as well as mining the currency itself.

China has mixed feelings about Bitcoin.

On one hand, the government worries that Bitcoin will allow Chinese people to bypass its strict limits on how much money they can send abroad, and could also be used to commit crimes. Chinese officials are moving to close Bitcoin exchanges, where the currency is bought and sold, though they have not set a time frame. While that would not affect Bitcoin manufacturing directly, it would make buying and selling Bitcoin more expensive in one of its major markets, potentially hurting prices.

On the other hand, the digital currency may represent an opportunity for China to push into new technologies, a motivation behind its

The Bitmain farm in Dalad Banner.

extensive push into other cutting-edge areas, like driverless cars and artificial intelligence. China continues to offer Bitcoin makers like Bitmain cheap electricity — making Bitcoin requires immense amounts of power — and other inducements.

Dalad Banner may be far away from Beijing's internet start-up scene and southern China's gadget hub. Still, many of the workers and surrounding residents see a digital opportunity for Dalad Banner and the rest of their part of Inner Mongolia, an area famous in China for half-finished factories and towns so empty that they are sometimes called ghost cities.

"Now the mine has about 50 employees," said Wang Wei, the manager of Bitmain China's Dalad Banner facility, using one of several metaphors for the work being done there. "I feel in the future it might bring hundreds or even thousands of jobs, like the big factories."

Mr. Wang, a 36-year-old resident and former coal salesman, purchased one Bitcoin about six months ago. It has since more than doubled in value. "I made quite a lot of money," he said.

Plugs in a warehouse at the Bitmain farm.

China also sees a potential new source of jobs, particularly in underdeveloped places like Dalad Banner. The county of about 370,000 people on the edge of the vast Kubuqi Desert boasts coal reserves and coal-powered heavy industries like steel. But it lags behind much of the rest of the country in broadly developing its economy. It is part of the urban area of Ordos, a city about 350 miles away from Beijing famous for its empty buildings.

Dalad Banner is not the sort of place that at first glance looks like a home for high-tech work. Indeed, the idea took some getting used to, even among the workers.

"I didn't know anything about Bitcoin then," said Li Shuangsheng, a 28-year-old resident who maintains the operations of one of the eight factories.

He bounced from job to job — the chemical plant was too noisy and polluted, he said — before he landed about one month ago at Bitmain

China's Dalad Banner factory, one of the few lucrative job opportunities in the sparsely populated region.

Mr. Li does not yet own any Bitcoin, but he is happy with the work and studying up on the subject online when family time permits.

"Now," he said, "I'm starting to have some idea."

Many at the farm have experienced the ups and downs of the local economy.

Bai Xiaotu was laid off from a state-owned furniture factory in 1997. He had been doing different menial jobs until he went to work at Bitmain's Dalad Banner farm in December as a cleaner.

"Look around, there are abandoned factories on both sides of our farm," said Mr. Bai, a 53-year-old with a weather-beaten face. "Many factories are not doing that great."

But the industry is still new to most. Bai Dong, Mr. Bai's 31-year-old son, had never heard of Bitcoin when his father first got the job. After searching on the internet, he found that the Bitcoin price was rising quickly and that the farm was one of the biggest in the world. "I feel positive about the future of the industry," Mr. Bai said.

But he is still confused what Bitcoin mining is.

"We have coal mines," he said. "Now we have a Bitcoin mine. They are both mines. What's their relationship?"

Coinbase: The Heart of the Bitcoin Frenzy

BY NATHANIEL POPPER | DEC. 6, 2017

SAN FRANCISCO — The booming stock market of the 1920s had the New York Stock Exchange. The tech bubble of the 1990s had Nasdaq and E-Trade. And the virtual currency market of the last year has had Coinbase.

Coinbase has been at the center of the speculative frenzy driving up the value of Bitcoin — which topped $13,000 on Wednesday — and similar currencies. While there are many Bitcoin exchanges around the world, Coinbase has been the dominant place that ordinary Americans go to buy and sell virtual currency. No company had made it simpler to sign up, link a bank account or debit card, and begin buying Bitcoin.

The number of people with Coinbase accounts has gone from 5.5 million in January to 13.3 million at the end of November, according to data from the Altana Digital Currency Fund. In late November, Coinbase was sometimes getting 100,000 new customers a day — leaving the company with more customers than Charles Schwab and E-Trade.

The company faces challenges that are a reminder of the early days of now-mainstream online brokerages, which suffered through untimely outages and harsh criticism from traditional finance companies and government regulators. And Coinbase's missteps make it clear that the virtual currency industry is still young, with little of the battle testing that other financial markets have faced.

Coinbase's offices in downtown San Francisco show a start-up straining to keep up with growth. The company offers all the usual perks: free lunch and dinner, a sizable cafeteria and a room with yoga mats and board games.

Recently, every last inch of space has been pressed into action. The day after Bitcoin hit $10,000 last week, a training session for Coinbase

Coinbase employees lining up for free food in the gaming room of the company's office in San Francisco.

managers was moved to the game room because the engineering team needed to set up an emergency war room in the regular conference room.

The engineering team was trying to get Coinbase back up after the company's site was knocked offline, overwhelmed by a wave of incoming traffic. The number of visitors was double what it had been during the previous peak — two days earlier — and eight times what it had been in June, the peak until recently.

All of the big Bitcoin exchanges went down for at least part of the day, and Coinbase got back online faster than most. Still, any sort of downtime like that would be unacceptable in more traditional exchanges where stocks and commodities are traded.

"There are some well-known places this year when we weren't able to keep up with the volume," said Jeremy Henrickson, the chief product officer at Coinbase. "We are not where we need to be yet."

Most Friday afternoons, Brian Armstrong, the chief executive of Coinbase, holds a session in the cafeteria where employees can ask him anything. On the Friday of the record-hitting week, Mr. Armstrong discussed how the company was planning to grow and introduced Asiff Hirji, the new president and chief operating officer who will help him oversee it all.

The addition of Mr. Hirji, who had the same role at TD Ameritrade, was an implicit recognition that this new industry needs more seasoned hands to help young executives like Mr. Armstrong, who is 34. Mr. Hirji will manage Coinbase's trading operations while Mr. Armstrong focuses on new projects.

Mr. Armstrong has been running Coinbase since he co-founded it in 2012. Soft-spoken and reserved, he is an unusual figure in an industry filled with loud ideologues. He has done few public appearances during Bitcoin's recent bull market, and he recognizes the current frenzy has come with downsides.

"It's probably a little bit too focused on the price or people trying to make money," Mr. Armstrong said last week. "The thing I'm passionate about with digital currency is the world having an open financial system."

There is some irony to the success that Mr. Armstrong has experienced as a result of Bitcoin's rising price. In 2015, he helped lead a push to get the Bitcoin network to expand so it could handle more transactions. That effort failed, and Mr. Armstrong said in a recent interview that Bitcoin "did break my heart a little bit." He said he now holds more of his wealth in a Bitcoin competitor, Ether, which Coinbase also offers to customers.

Most of the screens in the Coinbase offices show the performance of the company's servers and customer metrics — like the number of customers downloading its iPhone app. For a time last week, Coinbase was among the 10 most downloaded iPhone apps, ahead of Uber and Twitter.

There are a few screens, including one in the cafeteria, that show the price of Bitcoin, Litecoin and Ether, the three virtual currencies that Coinbase buys, sells and holds for customers. Litecoin was created by a former Coinbase employee and is often described as silver to Bitcoin's gold. The newer Ether, which lives on the Ethereum network, is the second most valuable virtual currency after Bitcoin.

Coinbase set itself apart from other early Bitcoin companies when it was one of the first to get a new, special license for virtual currency companies in New York, called the BitLicense.

In the last year, though, Coinbase's most notable interaction with the government came after the Internal Revenue Service asked the company to hand over all of its customer records. Bitcoin holders are supposed to pay taxes if they collect gains from selling coins, but the I.R.S. has said that only a few hundred people have done so each year.

Coinbase fought the broad request from the I.R.S. and last week, while the price was skyrocketing, announced an agreement to hand over only the records of customers who made transactions involving more than $20,000 of virtual currencies — around 3 percent of the company's customers.

In addition to the brokerage service for small investors, Coinbase also runs an exchange, called GDAX, tailored to larger investors.

GDAX is overseen by Adam White, a former Air Force officer and a graduate of Harvard Business School. The day Bitcoin hit $10,000, he was in New York speaking with big financial institutions that are looking into Bitcoin. Some companies are getting ready to begin trading Bitcoin futures contracts in December, when that activity becomes available on the Chicago Mercantile Exchange.

A year ago, his Wall Street outreach was difficult, but "it's all inbound now," Mr. White said.

Not surprisingly, Coinbase is on a building spree. It recently leased office space in New York that will handle the Wall Street business and a new service that holds virtual currencies for large customers. In San Francisco, the company is adding two new floors in the building where it now has one.

Still, the main concern among virtual currency investors is that Coinbase has not expanded fast enough. In May, the company was criticized by a customer who could not reach anyone at the company after his account was hacked.

Coinbase is trying to be more responsive. At the beginning of the year, the company had 24 employees providing customer support. It now has around 180, with most of them outsourced from a call center in Texas and an email response team in the Philippines. The cafeteria is often turned into a "Crypto Club" where new employees are taught the ins and outs of virtual currency.

Daniel Romero, the general manager of Coinbase, said he wanted to have 400 customer support employees by the first quarter of next year to provide phone support around the clock. But in the meantime, there is a 10-day backlog of service requests.

"When your customer support issues are that publicly bad, and you have your site go down when people want to be trading," it's a very humbling experience, Mr. Romero said.

How the Winklevoss Twins Found Vindication in a Bitcoin Fortune

BY NATHANIEL POPPER | DEC. 19, 2017

THE WINKLEVOSS TWINS have carved an unorthodox path toward fame in the American business world.

They went to Harvard University and then on to the Olympics as rowers. Along the way, they fought a legal battle with Mark Zuckerberg over the ownership of Facebook. In the Oscar-nominated movie, "The Social Network," they were portrayed as uptight gentry, outwitted by the brilliant, budding tech mogul.

Cameron, the left-handed Winklevoss brother, and Tyler, the right-handed one, followed that with a risky bet: They used money from a $65 million settlement with Mr. Zuckerberg to load up on Bitcoin. That turned them into the first prominent virtual currency millionaires in 2013, back when Bitcoin was primarily known as a currency for online drug dealers.

More than a few people in Silicon Valley and on Wall Street saw the towering twins as the naïve — if chiseled — faces of the latest tulip bulb mania. Many still do.

But the soaring value of Bitcoin in recent months is giving the brothers a moment of vindication, and quite a bit more than that: Their Bitcoin stockpile was worth around $1.3 billion on Tuesday.

"We've turned that laughter and ridicule into oxygen and wind at our back," said Tyler Winklevoss in an interview last week.

It is unclear how fleeting their vindication, or their fortune, will be. Many Bitcoin aficionados are expecting a major correction to the recent spike in its value, which has gone from $1,000 for one coin at the beginning of the year to around $18,500 on Tuesday.

If nothing else, the growing fortune of the 36-year-old Winklevoss twins is a reminder that for all the small investors getting into Bitcoin this year, the biggest winners have been a relatively small number of early holders who had plenty of money to start with and have been riding a price roller coaster for years. (The mysterious creator of Bitcoin, Satoshi Nakamoto, is believed by researchers to be holding onto Bitcoin worth around $19 billion.)

Some of these new Bitcoin millionaires are cashing out and buying Lamborghinis, professional hockey teams or even low-risk bond funds. The Winklevoss twins, though, said they had no intention to diversify.

"We still think it is probably one of the best investments in the world and will be for the decades to come," Tyler Winklevoss said. "And if it's not, we'd rather live with disappointment than regret."

They have collected an additional $350 million or so of other virtual currencies, most of it in the Bitcoin alternative called Ethereum. The brothers are also majority owners of the virtual currency exchange they founded, Gemini, which likely takes their joint holdings to a value well over $2 billion, or enough to make each of them a billionaire.

They have sold almost none of their original holdings. While they each have apartments in downtown Manhattan, they say they live relatively spartan lives with few luxuries. Cameron drives an old S.U.V.; Tyler doesn't have a car at all.

The Winklevoss twins' financial rise began during their settlement with Mr. Zuckerberg in 2008. Their lawyers urged them to take the $45 million (after lawyers' fees) in cash. But they wanted to be paid in shares of Facebook.

"The lawyers thought we were crazy," Cameron Winklevoss said last week. "We thought they were crazy for taking cash."

By the time Facebook went public in 2012, their stock was worth around $300 million, their rowing careers were over, and they were looking for something new.

When they began buying Bitcoin in late 2012, the price of an individual coin was below $10. Few people in Silicon Valley or on Wall Street had publicly expressed interest in the virtual currency.

The Winklevoss twins sit in on a daily meeting at Gemini in New York City.

Over a few months, the brothers bought one percent of all the outstanding Bitcoin at the time — or some 120,000 tokens. As they did, the price soared, making their Bitcoin portfolio worth around $11 million by the time they went public with it in April 2013.

Their buying spree was mocked at the time, and a few of their early decisions fueled that derision. They also invested in Bitinstant, one of the first companies to trade bitcoins online. Bitinstant's executives, in fact, had tutored the brothers in the basics of Bitcoin.

The chief executive of Bitinstant, Charlie Shrem, was arrested in 2014, accused of helping to supply bitcoins to users of online drug markets. Mr. Shrem pleaded guilty to lesser charges and was sentenced to a year in jail. The Winklevosses were never implicated in the wrongdoing, which happened before they became investors.

While that drama was unfolding, the twins applied to create the first Bitcoin exchange traded fund, or E.T.F., an investment product that would hold bitcoins but be traded on stock exchanges. That brought more criticism from people who wondered why someone would buy a fund rather than Bitcoin itself. Earlier this year, regulators rejected the application.

On top of all that, until last year the price of Bitcoin was sliding and the virtual currency concept was looking wobbly. But the Winklevosses, who once bet that years of punishing rowing practices would take them to the Olympics, held their ground.

"We are very comfortable in very high-risk environments with absolutely no guarantee of success," Tyler Winklevoss said. "I don't mean existing in that environment for days, weeks or months. I mean, year after year."

They sold some of their tokens to pay for Gemini, a name that means twins in Latin. Like the Bitcoin E.T.F., their investment in Gemini was driven by their experience with the difficulty of buying and securely storing Bitcoin.

Every Bitcoin sits in an address that can only be accessed with the corresponding password, or private key. The problem with this system is that anyone who gets hold of a private key can easily take the Bitcoin. And unlike money taken from a bank account, stolen Bitcoin are essentially impossible to retrieve. A number of virtual currency exchanges and wallets have collectively lost billions of dollars worth of Bitcoin to thieves.

The Winklevosses came up with an elaborate system to store and secure their own private keys. They cut up printouts of their private keys into pieces and then distributed them in envelopes to safe deposit boxes around the country, so if one envelope were stolen the thief would not have the entire key.

With Gemini, they have created a high-tech version of this process to hold customer money. Getting into the company's wallets requires multiple signatures from cryptographically sealed devices that were never linked to the internet.

Gemini got a license from New York State regulators that allows them to hold bitcoins for regulated banks and asset managers —

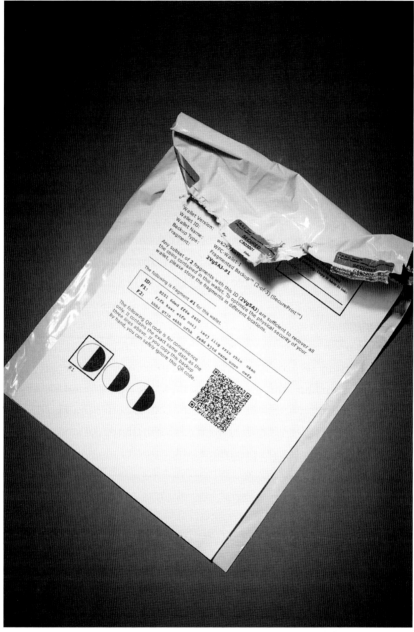

VINCENT TULLO FOR THE NEW YORK TIMES

The Winklevoss brothers recorded parts of the security code for their Bitcoin on papers stored in safe deposit boxes around the country.

something essentially no other virtual currency companies can do. That has turned Gemini into one of the most trusted destinations for sophisticated investors.

"Gemini is an underappreciated exchange, one of the few exchanges I trust as a custodian," said Ari Paul, a managing partner at the virtual currency hedge fund BlockTower Capital.

Gemini is now expanding from its old 5,000-square-foot offices to new, 35,000-square-foot facilities in Midtown Manhattan.

This doesn't mean Gemini or the Winklevosses have ironed out all the kinks. Like many other exchanges, Gemini has struggled to stay online in the deluge of new customers in recent weeks.

These growing pains are part of the reason the brothers say they are holding onto their Bitcoin. They believe virtual currencies are still a long way from real mainstream adoption.

They said they might look at selling when the value of all the Bitcoin in circulation approaches the value of all gold in the world — some $7 trillion or $8 trillion compared with the $310 billion value of all Bitcoin on Tuesday — given that they think Bitcoin is set to replace gold as a rare commodity. But then Tyler Winklevoss questioned even that, pointing out the ways that he believes Bitcoin is better than gold.

"In a funny way, I'm not sure we'd even sell there," he said. "Bitcoin is more than gold — it's a programmable store of money. It may continue to innovate."

There Is Nothing Virtual About Bitcoin's Energy Appetite

BY NATHANIEL POPPER | JAN. 21, 2018

SAN FRANCISCO — Creating a new Bitcoin requires electricity. A lot of it.

In the virtual currency world this creation process is called "mining." There is no physical digging, since bitcoins are purely digital. But the computer power needed to create each digital token consumes at least as much electricity as the average American household burns through in two years, according to figures from Morgan Stanley and Alex de Vries, an economist who tracks energy use in the industry.

The total network of computers plugged into the Bitcoin network consumes as much energy each day as some medium-size countries — which country depends on whose estimates you believe. And the network supporting Ethereum, the second-most valuable virtual currency, gobbles up another country's worth of electricity each day.

The energy consumption of these systems has risen as the prices of virtual currencies have skyrocketed, leading to a vigorous debate among Bitcoin and Ethereum enthusiasts about burning so much electricity.

The creator of Ethereum, Vitalik Buterin, is leading an experiment with a more energy-efficient way to create tokens, in part because of his concern about the impact that the network's electricity use could have on global warming.

"I would personally feel very unhappy if my main contribution to the world was adding Cyprus's worth of electricity consumption to global warming," Mr. Buterin said in an interview.

But many virtual currency aficionados argue that the energy consumption is worth it for the grander cause of securing the Bitcoin and Ethereum networks and making a new kind of financial infrastructure, free from the meddling of banks or governments.

"The electricity usage is really essential," said Peter Van Valkenburgh, the director of research at Coin Center, a group that advocates for virtual currency technology. "Because of the costs, we know the only people participating are serious, that they are economically invested. That creates the incentives for cooperation."

This dispute has its foundations in the complex systems that produce tokens like Bitcoin; Ether, the currency on the Ethereum network; and many other new virtual currencies.

All of the computers trying to mine tokens are in a computational race, trying to find a particular, somewhat random answer to a math algorithm. The algorithm is so complicated that the only way to find the desired answer is to make lots of different guesses. The more guesses a computer makes, the better its chances of winning. But each time the computers try new guesses, they use computational power and electricity.

The lure of new bitcoins encourages people to use lots of fast computers, and lots of electricity, to find the right answer and unlock the new bitcoins that are distributed every 10 minutes or so.

This process was defined by the original Bitcoin software, released in 2009. The goal was to distribute new coins to people on the Bitcoin network without a central institution handing out the money.

Early on, it was possible to win the contest with just a laptop computer. But the rules of the network dictate that as more computers join in the race, the algorithm automatically adjusts to get harder, requiring anyone who wants to compete to use more computers and more electricity.

These days, the 12.5 bitcoins that are handed out every 10 minutes or so are worth about $145,000, so people have been willing to invest astronomical sums to participate in this race, which has in turn made the race harder. This explains why there are now enormous server farms around the world dedicated to mining Bitcoin.

This process is central to Bitcoin's existence because in the process of mining, all the computers are also serving as accountants for the Bitcoin network. The algorithm the computers solve requires them to also keep track of all the new transactions coming onto the network.

The mining race is meant to be hard so that no one can dominate the accounting and fudge the records. In the 2008 paper that first described Bitcoin, the mysterious creator of the virtual currency, Satoshi Nakamoto, wrote that the system was designed to thwart a "greedy attacker" who might want to alter the records and "defraud people by stealing back his payments." Because of the mining and accounting rules, the attacker "ought to find it more profitable to play by the rules."

The rules have kept attackers at bay in the nine years since the network got going. Without this process, most computer scientists agree, Bitcoin would not work.

But there is disagreement over the real value of Bitcoin and the network that supports it.

For people who consider Bitcoin nothing more than a speculative bubble — or a speculative bubble that has enabled online drug sales and ransom payments — any new contribution toward global warming is probably not worth it.

But Bitcoin aficionados counter that it has allowed for the creation of the first financial network with no government or company in charge. In countries like Zimbabwe and Argentina, Bitcoin has sometimes provided a more stable place to park money than the local currency. And in countries with more stable economies, Bitcoin has led to a flurry of new investments, jobs and start-up companies.

"Labeling Bitcoin mining as a 'waste' is a failure to look at the big picture," Marc Bevand, a miner and analyst, wrote on his blog. The jobs alone, he added, "are a direct, measurable and positive impact that Bitcoin already made on the economy."

But even some people who are interested in all that innovation have worried about the enormous electrical use.

Mr. de Vries, who keeps track of the use on the site Digiconomist, estimated that each Bitcoin transaction currently required 80,000 times more electricity to process than each Visa credit card transaction, for example.

"Visa is more centralized," Mr. de Vries said. "If you really distrust the financial system, maybe that is unattractive. But is that difference really worth the additional energy cost? I think for most people that is probably not worth the case."

The figures published by Mr. de Vries have been criticized by Mr. Bevand and other Bitcoin fans, who say they overstate the energy costs by a factor of about three. Many critics add that producing and securing physical money and gold also require lots of energy, in some cases as much as or more than Bitcoin uses.

Mr. Van Valkenburgh, of the Coin Center, has argued that Bitcoin miners, who can do the work anywhere, have an incentive to situate themselves near cheap, often green energy sources, especially now that coal-guzzling China appears to be exiting the mining business. Several mining companies have opened server farms near geothermal energy in Iceland and hydroelectric power in Washington State.

But the concerns about electricity use have still hit home with many in the industry. The virtual currencies known as Ripple and Stellar, which were created after Bitcoin, were designed not to require electrically demanding mining.

Perhaps the biggest change could come from the new mining process proposed by Mr. Buterin for Ethereum, a process that some smaller currencies are already using. Known as "proof of stake," it distributes new coins to people who are able to prove their ownership of existing coins — their stake in the system. The current method, which relies so heavily on computational power, is called "proof of work." Under that method, the accounts and people who get new coins don't need existing tokens. They just need lots of computers to take part in the computational race.

Energy concerns are not the only factor encouraging the move. Mr. Buterin also believes that the new method, which is likely to be rolled out over the next year, will allow for a less centralized network of computers overseeing the system.

But it is far from clear that the method will be as secure as the one used by Bitcoin. Mr. Buterin has been fiercely attacked by Bitcoin advocates, who say his proposal will lose the qualities that make virtual currencies valuable.

Mr. Van Valkenburgh said that for now, throwing lots of computing power into the mix — and the electricity that it burns — was the only proven solution to the problems Bitcoin solves.

"At the moment, if you want robust security, you need proof of work," he said.

CHAPTER 5

Alternative Coins in Cryptocurrency's Social Vision

After Bitcoin, other virtual currencies followed. These new coins showed a tailoring of the initial blockchain technology to different purposes: Ethereum promised new decentralized applications and "smart contracts," Ripple was designed with financial institutions in mind and other coins were specialized to other commercial niches. The creation of these new coins allowed for new forms of financing and investing, such as "initial coin offerings" and AI-powered investment firms, while restarting the conversation about the broader social vision of cryptocurrencies.

In Bitcoin's Orbit: Rival Virtual Currencies Vie for Acceptance

BY NATHANIEL POPPER | NOV. 24, 2013

FOR MANY PEOPLE, Bitcoin seems like something from the day after tomorrow.

For Lawrence Blankenship, it's already a thing of the past.

A software engineer from Springfield, Mo., Mr. Blankenship is putting his money on PeerCoin, one of the biggest of the virtual currencies that are being promoted as alternatives to Bitcoin.

With mounting interest from prominent investors and growing acceptance from regulators, Bitcoin — either the new gold or the next

Dutch tulip craze, depending on who is being asked — is at the center of the virtual money universe. Yet there are dozens of digital alternatives, like PeerCoin, Litecoin and anoncoin, whose backers point to advantages they say their currency has over Bitcoin.

PeerCoin, according to Mr. Blankenship, is closer than Bitcoin to the perfect, communal money. Mr. Blankenship, who is 34, has arranged to accept PeerCoin as the virtual currency of choice at a Star Trek convention he is organizing in his hometown.

"Looking down the road 10 years from now, I definitely see Bitcoin being ousted," he said. "Everyone's going to start switching to other coins, and hopefully PeerCoin comes out ahead in that."

In the alternative galaxy of virtual currencies, newly created money can become worth millions of real dollars in a few months. All the PeerCoin in existence, for example, was worth nearly $40 million last week. Programmers and mathematicians release new entrants into the field almost every week. On one popular exchange, Cryptsy, 60 different coins can now be traded.

Almost all of these altcoins, as they are known, have fed on the stratospheric rise of Bitcoin. Since the beginning of the month, the value of Bitcoin rose to more than $900 at one point, from $200, and it is up 6,000 percent since the beginning of the year.

Many of the altcoins have risen at the same clip, driven by bets that the Internet has room for more than one form of virtual money, or that Bitcoin can be overtaken. The constant innovation opens the door to new opportunities for fraud and illegal activities.

Thanks to a lack of regulation, pump-and-dump schemes have become common. But the thousands of hours being poured into these projects underscore the degree to which a small but growing community believes that it has found the future of money.

"It's a very intriguing thing, because in principle, you can have a kind of money with some advantages that have never been possessed by any past forms of money," said George Selgin, an economics professor at the University of Georgia at Athens.

If this is a contest, Bitcoin is still light-years ahead of any of its competitors — the value of all Bitcoin is measured in the billions of dollars, while only a few others have even cracked a hundred million. And Bitcoin has the basic attributes that most other coins are trying to imitate: an open-source computer code with no central authority and a mathematically determined rate of expansion, not relying on a central bank.

What's more, most altcoins share the biggest weakness of Bitcoin: a violently fluctuating value. Most people are willing to use real currencies because they have stable values that make them good units of exchange. Virtual currencies, these days, are more like speculative commodities.

But this is not stopping the ascent of things like Litecoin, which is generally viewed as the second-most-popular digital money, with a total value of about $250 million last week. Unlike Bitcoin, which was invented by a shadowy creator known only as Satoshi Nakamoto, Litecoin was created by Charles Lee, a 36-year-old former programmer at Google who lives with his wife and two children in Silicon Valley.

ALEXIS CUAREZMA FOR THE NEW YORK TIMES

Charles Lee, creator of Litecoin, at home in Mountain View, Calif. Unlike others, he had no hoard of coins upon its release.

Mr. Lee said he wrote the original code for Litecoin in the hours after his children had gone to sleep. At the time, he said, many of the new currencies were being created by people who kept large hoards of the money they created, and then cashed out as soon as it rose in value. Mr. Lee, by contrast, gave advance notice of Litecoin's release, and on that day he began with no coins himself.

Like Bitcoin, new Litecoin is created through a so-called mining process in which computers compete to solve math problems, with coins going to the first computer that succeeds.

The goal with Litecoin, Mr. Lee said, was not to replace Bitcoin. Instead, it was to be "silver to Bitcoin's gold," with faster-moving transactions and a more democratic mining process.

"People like choices," said Mr. Lee, who now works for Coinbase, a company that provides virtual currency wallets. "You want to diversify your crypto-currency investments."

Another virtual currency viewed as being in the top ranks is Ripple, which is at the center of a new online payment system also called Ripple. This has won some mainstream following because it has big Silicon Valley backers and promises to be more transparent and easier to regulate than Bitcoin.

Bitcoin has been criticized for the anonymity of its transactions, which have made it attractive for buying drugs and guns online. But many altcoin fans are more bothered by how easily governments can follow Bitcoin, because the transactions are all recorded on a public ledger. This was the motivation for the creators of anoncoin, which has been rising in value.

Not surprisingly, the person behind anoncoin's email address did not want to share his or her identity.

But the person, going by the name Meeh, said the team behind anoncoin was "just people trying to help people become anonymous in this over-surveillanced world."

PeerCoin, Mr. Blankenship's money of choice, also has a creator who refuses to be identified, going by the name Sunny King. In an

Internet chat, Sunny King said one of the goals with PeerCoin was to create money that did not require the same computer resources to mine — making it more environmentally sustainable. More recently, Sunny King released a second new currency, Primecoin, that forces miners to find new strings of prime numbers — a potentially valuable task for the mathematical world.

"We are not greedy," Sunny King said. "We think crypto-currency also needs moral character behind it."

Mr. Blankenship is pushing for Sunny King's currencies and so are some friends in Springfield. One of those friends, John Manglaviti, said he dedicated 30 hours a week to promoting PeerCoin, after his day job, and thinks it could be "right there as an alternative to Bitcoin."

First, though, he said, the "challenge is to take this out of the geek world and make it something my mom could use."

Ethereum, a Virtual Currency, Enables Transactions That Rival Bitcoin's

BY NATHANIEL POPPER | MARCH 27, 2016

A NEW VIRTUAL gold rush is underway.

Even as Bitcoin, riven by internal divisions, has struggled, a rival virtual currency — known as Ethereum — has soared in value, climbing 1,000 percent over the last three months.

Beyond the price spike, Ethereum is also attracting attention from giants in finance and technology, like JPMorgan Chase, Microsoft and IBM, which have described it as a sort of Bitcoin 2.0.

The rise of the relatively new virtual currency has been helped by a battle within the Bitcoin community over how the basic Bitcoin software should develop.

The fights have slowed down Bitcoin transactions and led some people to look for alternative virtual currencies to power their businesses. Enter Ethereum.

Like Bitcoin, the Ethereum system is built on a blockchain in which every transaction is recorded publicly. The promise of such a system is that it allows the exchange of money and assets more quickly and more cheaply than relying on a long chain of middlemen.

But Ethereum has also won fans with its promise to do much more than Bitcoin. In addition to the virtual currency, the software provides a way to create online markets and programmable transactions known as smart contracts.

The system is complicated enough that even people who know it well have trouble describing it in plain English. But one application in development would let farmers put their produce up for sale directly to consumers and take payment directly from consumers. There are already dozens of functioning applications built on Ethereum, enabling new ways to manage and pay for electricity, sports bets and even Ponzi schemes.

All of this work is still very early. The first full public version of the Ethereum software was recently released, and the system could face some of the same technical and legal problems that have tarnished Bitcoin.

Many Bitcoin advocates say Ethereum will face more security problems than Bitcoin because of the greater complexity of the software. Thus far, Ethereum has faced much less testing, and many fewer attacks, than Bitcoin. The novel design of Ethereum may also invite intense scrutiny by authorities given that potentially fraudulent contracts, like the Ponzi schemes, can be written directly into the Ethereum system.

But the sophisticated capabilities of the system have made it fascinating to some executives in corporate America. IBM said last year that it was experimenting with Ethereum as a way to control real world objects in the so-called Internet of things.

Microsoft has been working on several projects that make it easier to use Ethereum on its computing cloud, Azure.

COLE WILSON FOR THE NEW YORK TIMES

ConsenSys employees in Brooklyn. The company has hired more than 50 developers.

"Ethereum is a general platform where you can solve problems in many industries using a fairly elegant solution — the most elegant solution we have seen to date," said Marley Gray, a director of business development and strategy at Microsoft.

Mr. Gray is responsible for Microsoft's work with blockchains, the database concept that Bitcoin introduced. Blockchains are designed to store transactions and data without requiring any central authority or repository.

Blockchain ledgers are generally maintained and updated by networks of computers working together — somewhat similar to the way that Wikipedia is updated and maintained by all its users.

Many corporations, though, have created their own Ethereum networks with private blockchains, independent of the public system, and that could ultimately detract from the value of the individual unit in the Ethereum system — known as an Ether — that people have recently been buying.

The interest in Ethereum is one sign of the corporate fascination with blockchains. Most major banks have expressed an interest in using them to make trading and money transfer faster and more efficient. On Tuesday, executives from the largest banks will gather for a conference, "Blockchain: Tapping Into the Real Potential, Cutting Through the Hype."

Many of these banks have recently been looking at how some version of Ethereum might be put to use. JPMorgan, for instance, has created a specific tool, Masala, that allows some of its internal databases to interact with an Ethereum blockchain.

Michael Novogratz, a former top executive at the private equity firm Fortress Investing Group, who helped lead Fortress's investment in Bitcoin, has been looking at Ethereum since he left Fortress last fall. Mr. Novogratz said that he made a "significant" purchase of Ether in January. He has also heard how the financial industry's chatter about the virtual currency has evolved.

"A lot of the more established players were thinking, 'It's still an experiment,' " he said. "It feels like in the last two to three months that experiment is at least getting a lot more validation."

Since the beginning of the year, the value of an individual unit of Ether has soared as high as $12 from around $1. That has brought the value of all existing Ether to over $1 billion at times, significantly more than any virtual currency other than Bitcoin, which had over $6 billion in value outstanding last week.

Since Bitcoin was invented, there have been many so-called altcoins that have tried to improve on Bitcoin, but none have won the following of Ethereum.

Unlike Bitcoin, which was released in 2009 by a mysterious creator known as Satoshi Nakamoto, Ethereum was created in a more transparent fashion by a 21-year-old Russian-Canadian, Vitalik Buterin, after he dropped out of Waterloo University in Ontario.

The most basic aim of Ethereum was to make it possible to program binding agreements into the blockchain — the smart contract concept. Two people, for instance, could program a bet on a sports game directly into the Ethereum blockchain. Once the final score came in from a mutually agreed upon source — say, The Associated Press — the money would be automatically transferred to the winning party. Ether can be used as a currency in this system, but Ether are also necessary to pay for the network power needed to process the bet.

The Ethereum system has sometimes been described as a single shared computer that is run by the network of users and on which resources are parceled out and paid for by Ether.

A team of seven co-founders helped Mr. Buterin write up the software after he released the initial description of the system. Mr. Buterin's team raised $18 million in 2014 through a presale of Ether, which helped fund the Ethereum Foundation, which supports the software's development.

Like Bitcoin, Ethereum has succeeded by attracting a dedicated network of followers who have helped support the software, partly in the hope that their Ether will increase in value if the system succeeds. Last week, there were 5,800 computers — or nodes —

helping support the network around the world. The Bitcoin network had about 7,400 nodes.

One of Mr. Buterin's co-founders, Joseph Lubin, has set up ConsenSys, a company based in Brooklyn that has hired over 50 developers to build applications on the Ethereum system, including one that enables music distribution and another that allows for a new kind of financial auditing.

The ConsenSys offices are in an old industrial building in the Bushwick section of Brooklyn. The office is essentially one large room, with all the messy trademarks of a start-up operation, including white boards on the walls and computer parts lying around.

Mr. Lubin said he had thrown himself into Ethereum after starting to think that it delivered on some of the failed promise of Bitcoin, especially when it came to allowing new kinds of online contracts and markets.

"Bitcoin presented the broad strokes vision, and Ethereum presented the crystallization of how to deliver that vision," he said.

Joseph Bonneau, a computer science researcher at Stanford who studies so-called crypto-currencies, said Ethereum was the first system that had really caught his interest since Bitcoin.

It is far from a sure thing, he cautioned.

"Bitcoin is still probably the safest bet, but Ethereum is certainly No. 2, and some folks will say it is more likely to be around in 10 years," Mr. Bonneau said. "It will depend if any real markets develop around it. If there is some actual application."

Ripple Aims to Put Every Transaction on One Ledger

BY QUENTIN HARDY | APRIL 6, 2016

CHRIS LARSEN started with a vision of making it possible for, say, a goatherd in Central Asia to do business efficiently with a fisherman in Africa or a merchant in London.

But now he has tweaked the idea into something that could play a role in transforming the international financial system — and the world beyond.

"We're heading for a day when every device in the world might be an economic actor," said Mr. Larsen, who made a fortune as a pioneer in online lending and founded Ripple, an Internet technology company. "It starts by being in the sewer system of finance."

The big banks at the center of global money movement, coordinating cash transfers for companies paying overseas suppliers, would not enjoy the comparison to a network of underground tunnels and pipes that carry waste. Yet while mail, music and movies travel fast online, older-style money transactions remain slow, creaky and clogged. It can take days for someone in the United States to pay someone in Africa.

Ripple and several other companies working in the online world aim to fix that with a technology known by the yawn-producing term "distributed ledger."

Its possibilities are anything but dull, however: Mr. Larsen imagines that the technology could go far beyond accommodating financial transactions among people and eventually enable self-driving cars to pay for tolls, parking and fuel without the help of humans. Home energy meters with ledgers might buy different sources of energy. Jet engines could record the installation of new parts and pay for maintenance on the spot.

Like many things in tech, a distributed ledger is a seemingly complex idea that is actually built on a very simple one.

Since the dawn of record-keeping, ledgers have been where receipts and disbursements of cash and goods are recorded. If you buy a sandwich at a deli, for example, several ledgers come into play. The money you carry to pay for it registers a slight deduction on your personal ledger. The deli owner's ledger records a gain in one place and in another a payment for the ham it bought from a supplier. A ledger at the bank records the deposit it receives from the deli owner.

In a world where every business has its own books, payments tend to stop and start between different ledgers. An overseas transfer leaves the ledger of one business, then goes on another ledger at a domestic bank. It then might hit the ledger of a bank in the international transfer system. It travels to another bank in the foreign country, before ending up on the ledger of the company being paid.

Each time it moves to a different ledger, the money has a different identity, taking up time and potentially causing confusion. For some companies, it is a nightmare that can't end soon enough.

"Why should it take me 48 hours to make a foreign currency payment?" said David Morton, chief financial officer of Seagate Technology, a major manufacturer of computer data storage devices. "I have 10,000 suppliers and handle 100,000 invoices a month. If I could pay people immediately, what kind of a discount would I get?"

In other words, what if one ledger could be shared among all the people in a transaction, who would agree on a common database of value that would do away with the need for currency exchanges? The actions would be recorded securely, with each participant able to see only the parts he needed to see. None of the middlemen would be needed, and payments could happen much faster.

That is the idea behind a distributed ledger. Seagate has invested in Ripple and is testing the technology.

The distributed ledger is best known as the underlying system that makes possible Bitcoin, the stateless cryptocurrency. Bitcoin got a bad name as a wildly fluctuating currency for drug dealers and tax cheats, in part because its participants remained anonymous. But many banks and businesses say the underlying ledger technology, if it is secure and transparent, can be more efficient than our current methods.

"Banks are struggling with different regulations, fragmented systems and siloed practices," said Owen Jelf, global managing director for capital markets at Accenture, which has also worked with Ripple. "We're excited about this as a technology to make things more efficient."

Accenture has made several bets on the technology. Aside from Ripple, it has invested in the distributed ledger company Digital Asset Holdings, and it is working with clients in financial trading on using the technology.

Another distributed ledger platform, called Ethereum, works off the same technology that Bitcoin does, but it is run as an open-source software project, meaning the software code is freely available for anyone to work on.

Still another, the Hyperledger Project, recently received 44,000 lines of code from IBM, which is sharing some of its software with developers who are trying to create distributed ledgers. IBM also plans to deploy distributed ledgers internally in what would be a significant test, considering that the company does $45 billion in global financing each year.

There is even the ledger system Bigchain DB that is posited as a way to prevent blood diamonds — those sold to finance armed conflicts — from entering the international gems trade. (A distributed ledger can be set up to identify every actor and what they do.)

Ripple's technology is similar to the Bitcoin system, but with some differences that make it easy to manage a far larger number of transactions at the same time. Following Bitcoin's lead, Mr. Larsen also worked on developing his own currency, called XRP. But he later decided to incorporate XRP into his ledger technology as a way to improve the existing international system, instead of overwhelming it with a new cryptocurrency.

He appears to have decided he will have more success by working with authorities on the existing problems of global transactions than on a new currency like Bitcoin, whose fans favor major disruption. "A lot of financial technology is foolhardy," Mr. Larsen said. "Saying, 'We're going to kill banks. We're going to disrupt everything,' ignores some realities."

A San Francisco native, Mr. Larsen began his career conducting international audits for Chevron. He graduated from Stanford Graduate School of Business in 1991.

Five years later, he started E-Loan, one of the first online mortgage companies. He took it public, but left in 2005 to start Prosper Marketplace, a peer-to-peer lending operation that, after initial regulatory clashes over lending laws, has facilitated several billion dollars' worth of loans.

He left Prosper in 2012 to work on XRP and a global ledger system open to everyone trading anything that two people agreed was worth something — goats, money, labor, you name it.

He started Ripple, originally Ripple Labs, in 2013. In 2015, it paid a $700,000 civil fine for selling XRP without registering with the United States Financial Crimes Enforcement Network. Then Mr. Larsen abandoned his Internet currency plans and turned toward the bigger transactional system.

Perhaps in a sign that regulators agreed it was time to figure out how to move money in the networked world, Ripple was invited to the World Economic Forum in Davos, Switzerland, in January, where Mr. Larsen gave a presentation to central bankers from 40 countries.

Even die-hard Bitcoin fans seem ready to accept the idea that the most promising approach to reforming financial transactions — at least for now — is to focus on the system, rather than on a currency.

"What Chris and his team have done is to work within existing constraints," said Barry Silbert, founder of the Digital Currency Group, which has made 67 investments in financial technology businesses. "Longer term, we'll see if that can compete with an entirely new system."

A Venture Fund With Plenty of Virtual Capital, but No Capitalist

BY NATHANIEL POPPER | MAY 21, 2016

OLIVIER STERN, a 31-year-old French socialist with an appetite for risk, recently invested a third of his life savings — 10,000 euros, about $11,000 — in a cryptocurrency start-up that has no legal standing and runs head-on into regulatory obstacles, yet might very well upend the mysterious world of virtual investing.

The start-up, a sort of venture capital fund that calls itself the Decentralized Autonomous Organization, has essentially come out of nowhere in the last month and attracted about $152 million, at last count, from investors around the world like Mr. Stern — making it the most successful crowdfunded venture ever, by a significant margin.

The venture, like so many things related to the digital currencies that cryptographers are creating on the Internet, is difficult to describe, and it may not be legal. But thousands of mostly anonymous investors have already heard about it through word of mouth and sent money — in the form of Ether, a freshly coded form of currency that has held itself out as a new and improved version of Bitcoin, the most popular virtual scrip.

For these investors, in some sense it is the digital equivalent of buying into a bakery with no baker, no menu and no assurance that the ovens will even be delivered. But among the crowd that has invested, faith in the computer code that governs the project appears strong enough to override all those concerns.

After it collects Ether from investors — the deadline to buy in is May 28 — the D.A.O. aims to put the money into other digital currency start-ups. The investing decisions are to be made through online polling of shareholders like Mr. Stern, who has a day job dealing with parking policy in the town of Montreuil, just outside Paris.

"I think it is the beginning of something that could, in a way, make history," said Mr. Stern, who previously lost a small sum of money he invested in Bitcoin when a major Bitcoin exchange — Mt. Gox — went bust. "Maybe it can fail, maybe it can succeed, but for sure it is an idea that is very interesting."

The rise of the new venture comes at a time when the technology underlying virtual currencies is rapidly being embraced by the mainstream: Most Wall Street firms and many central banks are experimenting with the blockchain, the online ledger system that Bitcoin and Ether pioneered. Banks hope the blockchain, or something like it, can provide a faster, cheaper way of conducting transactions and storing data.

The D.A.O., on the other hand, returns to the more radical ambitions of virtual currencies. It is set up according to computer code, with no human executives. All decisions will be made by votes of the people who buy in — using software — making it a sort of technology-enabled leaderless collective.

PIERRE TERDJMAN FOR THE NEW YORK TIMES

Olivier Stern at his house in Montreuil, outside Paris. Mr. Stern has invested a third of his life savings in a start-up called the Decentralized Autonomous Organization.

The basic code was written by a 32-year-old German programmer, Christoph Jentzsch. But he is not set to have any continuing role, and the D.A.O. does not hold the money of investors; instead, the investors own D.A.O. tokens that give them rights to vote on potential projects. Mr. Jentzsch said on Wednesday in an interview that he thought the structure absolved him of any legal responsibility for what could happen with the project.

"Of course this venture is fraught with risks," Mr. Jentzsch said in an email. But he also predicted, "This technology represents the future of the Internet."

Experts on virtual currencies say that Mr. Jentzsch and others involved have stepped into dangerous regulatory legal territory. American regulators have previously come down hard on entrepreneurs who sold investments using virtual currencies.

Patrick Murck, a lawyer who has long dealt with Bitcoin issues, said that even if Mr. Jentzsch and his collaborators were not operating the venture, they could face legal liability for promoting it if the investments go awry — and, potentially, even if they don't.

"You can't code away your legal responsibilities," said Mr. Murck, who is a fellow at the Berkman Center for Internet & Society at Harvard. "This is something that has been tried before and has failed before."

As of Wednesday, an Ether was valued at $13 and a Bitcoin at $450 — evidence, perhaps, of the strangeness and subjectivity of these new currencies. The D.A.O.'s reliance on Ether has allowed people to send their money to it from anywhere in the world without providing any identifying information, a design that is already raising concerns about potential money laundering.

The D.A.O. has also faced difficult questions from virtual currency aficionados, who worry that the organization's code was put together relatively hastily without the sort of security testing that has preceded previous projects based on Ethereum, the technology platform that underpins Ether.

"It's an unstable thing right now," said Joseph Lubin, who was one of the founders of Ethereum. "Young, complex machines tend to have flaws and vulnerabilities that you can't anticipate."

Mr. Jentzsch acknowledged that he did not anticipate the venture growing to anything close to the size it has reached. The biggest similar projects have attracted a few million dollars.

"If I would have known the size it has grown to, maybe the tester in me would say, 'I need more testing,' " he said. "This is very risky. It's all new land."

So far, two projects have applied to the D.A.O. for funding. One of them is a company run by Mr. Jentzsch and his brother, Simon, that is creating a new kind of physical lock that can be controlled remotely through the Ethereum network, according to contracts written into the network.

The code that Mr. Jentzsch wrote for the organization has several safeguards that would make it hard for him or anyone else to game the voting of shareholders to win investments. But even successful crowdfunding sites do not have a great track record of harnessing the enthusiasm of users to pick good investments.

The creator of a now defunct crowdfunding site fueled by Bitcoin, BitShares, wrote a biting online post on Tuesday arguing that the D.A.O. would most likely fail for the same reason that BitShares ultimately failed: "people problems, economic problems and political problems."

"My opinion is that the D.A.O. will be D.O.A. (Dead on Arrival)," Daniel Larimer, the founder of BitShares, wrote. "The theory of jointly deciding to fund efforts will face the reality of individual self-interest, politics and economics."

The possibility of failure did not deter Mr. Stern, the Frenchman who put in the equivalent of $11,000. He said he thought the D.A.O. would provide a good financial return, but he was also motivated by his belief that the venture is an experiment in a new way of organizing companies, and potentially even governments.

"It's important for people to propose and try an alternative," he said.

Easiest Path to Riches on the Web? An Initial Coin Offering

BY NATHANIEL POPPER | JUNE 23, 2017

A NEW CROP of technology entrepreneurs is forgoing the usual routes to raising money. The entrepreneurs are not pitching venture capitalists, selling stock in an initial public offering or using crowdfunding sites like Kickstarter.

Instead, before they even have a working product, they are creating their own digital currencies and selling so-called coins on the web, sometimes raising tens of millions of dollars in a matter of minutes.

The pitch is that once the products are up and running, the currencies — with names like BAT, Mysterium and Siacoin — will be redeemable for services like data storage or anonymous internet access, and could appreciate in value in the meantime.

Known as initial coin offerings, this latest twist in online fundraising has made it easier than ever for entrepreneurs to raise large sums of money without dealing with the hassles of regulators, investor protections or accountants.

Since the beginning of the year, 65 projects have raised $522 million in these offerings, according to Smith & Crown, a research firm focused on the new industry.

It is a frothy, sprawling and completely unregulated way of funding start-ups, leaving even veteran technology watchers scratching their heads.

"It's kind of like when you are a little kid and you know you are getting away with something," said Chris Burniske, an industry analyst at ARK Invest. "It's not going to last forever, but it's fun in the interim. The space is giddy right now."

Last month, a small team of computer engineers in Lithuania raised $14 million in 45 minutes by selling a coin, known as Mysterium, that is intended to give access to an encrypted online data service that is still being built.

The next day, a group of coders in the Bay Area pulled in $35 million in under 30 seconds of online fund-raising. The coders were offering Basic Attention Tokens, which will one day work on a new kind of ad-free web browser.

Then this week, a team in Switzerland raised around $100 million for a coin that will be used on an online chat program that has not yet been released, known as Status.

Proponents of initial coin offerings hail them as a financial innovation that empowers developers and gives early investors a chance to share in the profits of a successful new enterprise. But where some see a new method of crowdfunding online projects, critics say the phenomenon is ripe for abuse and, in many cases, a violation of American securities law.

"It's exploitative and abusive of the investing public," Preston Byrne, a technology lawyer specializing in virtual currencies, said about the offerings.

Last year, the first blockbuster coin offering, the Decentralized Autonomous Organization, quickly raised more than $150 million. But the project blew up after a hacker manipulated the code and stole more than $50 million worth of digital currency. A number of other projects since then have been labeled scams.

Even among supporters, many say there has been too much money pouring into unproven projects in recent months.

Fred Wilson, a founder of the venture capital firm Union Square Ventures, said he was "long term very bullish" on these new digital currencies. But he said, "We see many reasons to be cautious right now."

"There is a gold rush mentality in the sector right now and many people are doing the wrong things for the wrong reasons," he said.

Underpinning the surge in initial coin offerings is a broader boom in digital money. Bitcoin and Ether, two of the most popular virtual currencies, have soared in value in recent months. And when entrepreneurs sell new coins, they are asking for payment in Bitcoin or Ether, not United States dollars.

This means that conventional banks and financial institutions are essentially shut out, allowing initial coin offerings to take place beyond the control of regulators.

Among the people tossing their money into the pot is Pete Sussman, 27, a software developer at a St. Louis company called Fusion Marketing.

Mr. Sussman began with around $800 worth of Bitcoin, which he earned selling art and blog posts online. He used his Bitcoin first to invest in a project called BitShares. Then he bought into the Ethereum virtual currency, Ether. As the value of Ether soared over the last year, Mr. Sussman got a return of 1,000 percent on his original money.

In March, he used his Ether to buy a new virtual currency known as GNT, which was created as part of a project known as Golem, based in Poland. The value of GNT has jumped 3,000 percent in recent months, pushing the value of Mr. Sussman's digital currency to over $200,000.

Pete Sussman, front, interested his co-workers in St. Louis in digital currencies.

Along with GNT, other new tokens including Ark, Antshares and Spectrecoin have appreciated by more than 6,000 percent since they were issued.

Mr. Sussman has also had some bad moments along the way, such as the time that he sent what would now be $100,000 worth of Ether to a scammer who put up a fake digital address for another coin offering.

"I was at work. I went to the bathroom and I tried to throw up but nothing came out," Mr. Sussman said. "Then after a little bit, I went home and sulked."

When he told his co-workers about the experience, they did not warn him off the investments. Instead, they became excited about the trend. Now, half a dozen of his colleagues, including his boss, have a chat room where they discuss potential coin investments.

The projects selling coins come in several forms. Some are straightforward start-ups that design their coins like stock, with promised dividend payments if the company does well. Others are Bitcoin or Ethereum knockoffs, which the inventors sell in advance before launching to the public.

But most of the prominent projects are not traditional start-ups. Instead, the programmers are building online services similar to Wikipedia, which are intended to be open source and owned by no one.

The coins will become the internal payment method on these services once they are built — paying for computing power in the case of Golem, or file storage with a project called Storj. The sale of the coins will be used to compensate the programmers.

Even some well-established Silicon Valley names are using coins to raise funds. Brendan Eich, a co-founder of the Mozilla web browser project, is developing a new browser called Brave.

It was Mr. Eich who raised $35 million in just 30 seconds by selling millions of Basic Attention Tokens, or BAT, in late May. People using the Brave browser will be able to use their BAT to view web pages ad-free, and companies will be able to pay viewers for looking at ads. (The New York Times and other publishers have called Brave's ad-blocking technology illegal.)

The hope with a token like BAT is that as more people use the browser and more advertisers want the coins, the coins will become more sought after and the users will benefit from the rising price. These so-called network effects can also encourage users to get their friends to use a service.

Mr. Eich said he was anticipating that all the people holding tokens "will drive millions of users to join our ecosystem."

That is the dream. For now, several projects are raising millions without even having any computer code to test. And because of the lack of investor protections, the projects remain vulnerable to the whims of entrepreneurs, who could run away with their quick hauls of digital currency.

The most immediate problems could arise if regulators decide that the tokens being sold are unregistered securities, a violation of the law. An official with the Securities and Exchange Commission suggested at a conference last month that the agency was aware of the potential for problems and was looking at the market.

For at least some investors, such as Mr. Sussman, the possibility of big losses is the flip side of the big gains, and part of the allure.

"It's very Wild West," he said. "It's very easy to get into a situation where you can send things to a scammer very easily, and there is no recourse for it. That's kind of the beauty of it, too."

Some Bitcoin Backers Are Defecting to Create a Rival Currency

BY NATHANIEL POPPER | JULY 25, 2017

SAN FRANCISCO — For the last two years, rival factions have been vying for control of the Bitcoin virtual currency and its global network of computers and supporters.

Now, one of the main camps is preparing to break off and create a competing version of Bitcoin.

A group of investors and entrepreneurs, most of them based in Asia, have announced a plan to create what they are calling Bitcoin Cash, starting next week.

The plan would seal a divorce between opponents in a long-simmering feud over what Bitcoin should be — and lead to two competing virtual currencies going by the name of Bitcoin.

"I actually think it would be a good thing if there is a split," said Roger Ver, a Tokyo-based investor who voiced his preliminary support for Bitcoin Cash on Tuesday.

He said the differences among the different camps had quite likely grown too stark for them to move forward together.

Bitcoin Cash could easily dissolve into irrelevance — the level of support for it is still unclear — but the concrete plans to move forward have underscored, once again, how hard it is to govern a decentralized, open-source technology like Bitcoin with no single set of leaders or ownership.

"In the long run it will be forced to develop some real political structure to take these kinds of decisions, but it just isn't there yet, so the result has been chaos," said Joseph Bonneau, who has studied Bitcoin and is a fellow at the Electronic Frontier Foundation, which describes itself as a nonprofit defending digital privacy, free speech and innovation.

The Bitcoin divide is part of a wider splintering of the world that has sprung up around virtual currencies.

Many people who initially got excited about the unique technology behind Bitcoin have taken advantage of the public, open-source nature of the technology and created their own new virtual currencies, like Ethereum, Ripple and Litecoin. These other systems run according to different rules than Bitcoin, with some emphasizing more speed and complexity, and some more focused on anonymity and security.

The divisions have, if anything, increased the excitement and the value of all the virtual currencies in the world — and banks and governments have announced their own projects to harness the technology.

The price of Bitcoin has recently been at record highs, near $3,000, and several other coins have grown to be worth billions of dollars on their own. A whole class of companies have raised money in recent months by creating and selling their own new digital tokens.

Until now, though, Bitcoin has remained the most valuable digital token of them all, and it has kept its followers united by a single set of rules, despite all the warring behind the scenes.

The divisions, though, appear to have grown too stark to keep everyone on the same blockchain, as the ledger of all Bitcoin transactions is known.

Mr. Ver has been one of the leaders of a contingent that has long wanted to change the rules governing the Bitcoin network so that it can handle more transactions and compete with the likes of PayPal and Visa.

Bitcoin Cash is set to increase the limit on the number of transactions that can be processed by the Bitcoin network every 10 minutes. Currently, the network can process only blocks of transactions that are smaller than one megabyte, which allows for roughly five transactions in a second.

The move to increase the size of the so-called blocks, though, has run up against intense opposition from the programmers who maintain the Bitcoin software.

These programmers, known as the core developers, have said that increasing the amount of data included in each block of transactions would make it harder for individual users to process the blocks and easier for a small number of companies to take control of the Bitcoin network.

"It destroys the Bitcoin ethos, which is open and permissionless, where nobody is telling you what to do," said Samson Mow, the chief strategy officer at Blockstream, a company that employs some of the most prominent core developers.

The core developers have come up with their own solution to increase the number of transactions flowing through the system with software known as Segregated Witness, or SegWit. Mr. Ver and others, though, have said SegWit does not expand Bitcoin fast enough to keep up with its recent growth in popularity.

The arguments have given way to vicious mudslinging and hacking attacks against the leaders on both sides, leading some prominent developers to leave the project.

Proponents of increasing the block size, like Mr. Ver, have put forward proposals in the past that have failed to garner majority support in the community, in part because of concerns about the sophistication of the programmers working on the projects.

But the big block camp has not, until now, announced a definite plan to split off from the rest of Bitcoin.

While Bitcoin Cash will not exist until next week, a small number of exchanges have begun trading futures contracts, tied to the expected price of Bitcoin Cash. On Tuesday, it was trading around $450, or a fraction of the $2,600 value of an ordinary Bitcoin.

As recently as last week, it appeared that the major Bitcoin players had found a compromise that would avert a split in the network, or a fork as it is known in Bitcoin world.

Many of the largest Bitcoin companies agreed in May that they would install the SegWit software the core developers created, while also moving toward a doubling of the size of each block of transactions, to two megabytes, in November.

The largest Bitcoin processors had signaled last week that they intended to begin running the new software on Aug. 1. But the developers have suggested that they do not intend to move forward with any increase in the size of the blocks in the coming months.

One of Mr. Ver's many investment holdings, Bitcoin.com, announced on Tuesday that it would put all of its resources behind Bitcoin Cash if the block size has not been doubled by November.

To gain traction more broadly, Bitcoin Cash will have to win backing from the broader community of so-called Bitcoin miners.

Bitcoin miners are best known for using specialized computers to unlock, or mine, new Bitcoins. But miners also process Bitcoin transactions and have voting power over any changes to the Bitcoin network in direct proportion to the amount of computing power they dedicate to the network.

Most of the largest mining operations are now in China, thanks to the availability of cheap hardware and electricity.

One significant Chinese mining operation, ViaBTC, has been an outspoken supporter of Bitcoin Cash and has said it will begin backing the system next week.

The largest Bitcoin mining operator in the world, a company known as Bitmain, is a primary investor in ViaBTC. That has led many in the Bitcoin world to expect that Bitmain will also provide backing to Bitcoin Cash. But Bitmain has so far said only that it does not "rule out" supporting Bitcoin Cash.

When Bitcoin Cash comes into existence, every current holder of Bitcoins will have access to an equivalent amount of Bitcoin Cash, but from that point forward the two systems will diverge.

In the coming weeks, Bitcoin enthusiasts on all sides of the debate will be watching closely to see which big Bitcoin companies offer support for people who want to hold, trade and mine Bitcoin Cash.

Beyond the Bitcoin Bubble

BY STEVEN JOHNSON | JAN. 16, 2018

> layer innocent nothing argue pottery winner cotton menu task slim
> merge maid

THE SEQUENCE OF WORDS is meaningless: a random array strung together by an algorithm let loose in an English dictionary. What makes them valuable is that they've been generated exclusively for me, by a software tool called MetaMask. In the lingo of cryptography, they're known as my seed phrase. They might read like an incoherent stream of consciousness, but these words can be transformed into a key that unlocks a digital bank account, or even an online identity. It just takes a few more steps.

On the screen, I'm instructed to keep my seed phrase secure: Write it down, or keep it in a secure place on your computer. I scribble the 12 words onto a notepad, click a button and my seed phrase is transformed into a string of 64 seemingly patternless characters:

> 1b0be2162cedb2744d016943bb14e71de6af95a63af3790d6b41b1e719dc5c66

This is what's called a "private key" in the world of cryptography: a way of proving identity, in the same, limited way that real-world keys attest to your identity when you unlock your front door. My seed phrase will generate that exact sequence of characters every time, but there's no known way to reverse-engineer the original phrase from the key, which is why it is so important to keep the seed phrase in a safe location.

That private key number is then run through two additional transformations, creating a new string:

> 0x6c2ecd6388c550e8d99ada34a1cd55bedd052ad9

That string is my address on the Ethereum blockchain.

Ethereum belongs to the same family as the cryptocurrency Bitcoin, whose value has increased more than 1,000 percent in just the past year. Ethereum has its own currencies, most notably Ether, but the platform has a wider scope than just money. You can think of my Ethereum address as having elements of a bank account, an email address and a Social Security number. For now, it exists only on my computer as an inert string of nonsense, but the second I try to perform any kind of transaction — say, contributing to a crowdfunding campaign or voting in an online referendum — that address is broadcast out to an improvised worldwide network of computers that tries to verify the transaction. The results of that verification are then broadcast to the wider network again, where more machines enter into a kind of competition to perform complex mathematical calculations, the winner of which gets to record that transaction in the single, canonical record of every transaction ever made in the history of Ethereum. Because those transactions are registered in a sequence of "blocks" of data, that record is called the blockchain.

The whole exchange takes no more than a few minutes to complete. From my perspective, the experience barely differs from the usual routines of online life. But on a technical level, something miraculous is happening — something that would have been unimaginable just a decade ago. I've managed to complete a secure transaction without any of the traditional institutions that we rely on to establish trust. No intermediary brokered the deal; no social-media network captured the data from my transaction to better target its advertising; no credit bureau tracked the activity to build a portrait of my financial trustworthiness.

And the platform that makes all this possible? No one owns it. There are no venture investors backing Ethereum Inc., because there is no Ethereum Inc. As an organizational form, Ethereum is far closer to a democracy than a private corporation. No imperial chief executive calls the shots. You earn the privilege of helping to steer Ethereum's ship of state by joining the community and doing the work.

Like Bitcoin and most other blockchain platforms, Ethereum is more a swarm than a formal entity. Its borders are porous; its hierarchy is deliberately flattened.

Oh, one other thing: Some members of that swarm have already accumulated a paper net worth in the billions from their labors, as the value of one "coin" of Ether rose from $8 on Jan. 1, 2017, to $843 exactly one year later.

You may be inclined to dismiss these transformations. After all, Bitcoin and Ether's runaway valuation looks like a case study in irrational exuberance. And why should you care about an arcane technical breakthrough that right now doesn't feel all that different from signing in to a website to make a credit card payment?

But that dismissal would be shortsighted. If there's one thing we've learned from the recent history of the internet, it's that seemingly esoteric decisions about software architecture can unleash profound global forces once the technology moves into wider circulation. If the email standards adopted in the 1970s had included public-private key cryptography as a default setting, we might have avoided the cataclysmic email hacks that have afflicted everyone from Sony to John Podesta, and millions of ordinary consumers might be spared routinized identity theft. If Tim Berners-Lee, the inventor of the World Wide Web, had included a protocol for mapping our social identity in his original specs, we might not have Facebook.

The true believers behind blockchain platforms like Ethereum argue that a network of distributed trust is one of those advances in software architecture that will prove, in the long run, to have historic significance. That promise has helped fuel the huge jump in cryptocurrency valuations. But in a way, the Bitcoin bubble may ultimately turn out to be a distraction from the true significance of the blockchain. The real promise of these new technologies, many of their evangelists believe, lies not in displacing our currencies but in replacing much of what we now think of as the internet, while at the same time returning the online world to a more decentralized and egalitarian system. If you believe the evangelists, the blockchain is the future. But it is also a way of getting back to the internet's roots.

ONCE THE INSPIRATION for utopian dreams of infinite libraries and global connectivity, the internet has seemingly become, over the past year, a universal scapegoat: the cause of almost every social ill that confronts us. Russian trolls destroy the democratic system with fake news on Facebook; hate speech flourishes on Twitter and Reddit; the vast fortunes of the geek elite worsen income equality. For many of us who participated in the early days of the web, the last few years have felt almost postlapsarian. The web had promised a new kind of egalitarian media, populated by small magazines, bloggers and self-organizing encyclopedias; the information titans that dominated mass culture in the 20th century would give way to a more decentralized system, defined by collaborative networks, not hierarchies and broadcast channels. The wider culture would come to mirror the peer-to-peer architecture of the internet itself. The web in those days was hardly a utopia — there were financial bubbles and spammers and a thousand other problems — but beneath those flaws, we assumed, there was an underlying story of progress.

Last year marked the point at which that narrative finally collapsed. The existence of internet skeptics is nothing new, of course; the difference now is that the critical voices increasingly belong to former enthusiasts. "We have to fix the internet," Walter Isaacson, Steve Jobs's biographer, wrote in an essay published a few weeks after Donald Trump was elected president. "After 40 years, it has begun to corrode, both itself and us." The former Google strategist James Williams told The Guardian: "The dynamics of the attention economy are structurally set up to undermine the human will." In a blog post, Brad Burnham, a managing partner at Union Square Ventures, a top New York venture-capital firm, bemoaned the collateral damage from the quasi monopolies of the digital age: "Publishers find themselves becoming commodity content suppliers in a sea of undifferentiated content in the Facebook news feed. Websites see their fortunes upended by small changes in Google's search algorithms. And manu-facturers watch helplessly as sales dwindle when Amazon decides to source products directly in China and redirect demand to their own products." (Full disclosure: Burnham's firm invested in a company I started in 2006; we have had no financial relationship since it sold in 2011.) Even Berners-Lee, the inventor of the web itself, wrote a blog post voicing his concerns that the advertising-based model of social media and search engines creates a climate where "misinformation, or 'fake news,' which is surprising, shocking or designed to appeal to our biases, can spread like wildfire."

For most critics, the solution to these immense structural issues has been to propose either a new mindfulness about the dangers of these tools — turning off our smartphones, keeping kids off social media — or the strong arm of regulation and antitrust: making the tech giants subject to the same scrutiny as other industries that are vital to the pub-lic interest, like the railroads or telephone networks of an earlier age. Both those ideas are commendable: We probably should develop a new set of habits governing how we interact with social media, and it seems entirely sensible that companies as powerful as Google and Facebook should face the same regulatory scrutiny as, say, television networks. But those interventions are unlikely to fix the core problems that the online world confronts. After all, it was not just the antitrust division of the Department of Justice that challenged Microsoft's monopoly power in the 1990s; it was also the emergence of new software and hardware — the web, open-source software and Apple products — that helped under-mine Microsoft's dominant position.

The blockchain evangelists behind platforms like Ethereum believe that a comparable array of advances in software, cryptography and distributed systems has the ability to tackle today's digital problems: the corrosive incentives of online advertising; the quasi monopolies of Facebook, Google and Amazon; Russian misinformation campaigns. If they succeed, their creations may challenge the hegemony of the tech giants far more effectively than any antitrust regulation. They even claim to offer an alternative to the winner-take-all model of capitalism than has driven wealth inequality to heights not seen since the age of the robber barons.

That remedy is not yet visible in any product that would be intelligible to an ordinary tech consumer. The only blockchain project that has crossed over into mainstream recognition so far is Bitcoin, which is in the middle of a speculative bubble that makes the 1990s internet I.P.O. frenzy look like a neighborhood garage sale. And herein lies the cognitive dissonance that confronts anyone trying to make sense of the blockchain: the potential power of this would-be revolution is being actively undercut by the crowd it is attracting, a veritable goon squad of charlatans, false prophets and mercenaries. Not for the first time, technologists pursuing a vision of an open and decentralized network have found themselves surrounded by a wave of opportunists looking to make an overnight fortune. The question is whether, after the bubble has burst, the very real promise of the blockchain can endure.

TO SOME STUDENTS of modern technological history, the internet's fall from grace follows an inevitable historical script. As Tim Wu argued in his 2010 book, "The Master Switch," all the major information technologies of the 20th century adhered to a similar developmental pattern, starting out as the playthings of hobbyists and researchers motivated by curiosity and community, and ending up in the hands of multinational corporations fixated on maximizing shareholder value. Wu calls this pattern the Cycle, and on the surface at least, the internet has followed the Cycle with convincing fidelity. The internet began as a hodgepodge of government-funded academic research projects and side-hustle hobbies. But 20 years after the web first crested into the popular imagination, it has produced in Google, Facebook and Amazon — and indirectly, Apple — what may well be the most powerful and valuable corporations in the history of capitalism.

Blockchain advocates don't accept the inevitability of the Cycle. The roots of the internet were in fact more radically open and decentralized than previous information technologies, they argue, and had we managed to stay true to those roots, it could have remained that way. The online world would not be dominated by a handful of information-age titans; our news platforms would be less vulnerable to manipulation and fraud; identity theft would be far less common; advertising dollars would be distributed across a wider range of media properties.

To understand why, it helps to think of the internet as two fundamentally different kinds of systems stacked on top of each other, like layers in an archaeological dig. One layer is composed of the software protocols that were developed in the 1970s and 1980s and hit critical mass, at least in terms of audience, in the 1990s. (A protocol is the software version of a lingua franca, a way that multiple computers agree to communicate with one another. There are protocols that govern the flow of the internet's raw data, and protocols for sending email messages, and protocols that define the addresses of web pages.) And then above them, a second layer of web-based services — Facebook, Google, Amazon, Twitter — that largely came to power in the following decade.

The first layer — call it InternetOne — was founded on open protocols, which in turn were defined and maintained by academic researchers and international-standards bodies, owned by no one. In fact, that original openness continues to be all around us, in ways we probably don't appreciate enough. Email is still based on the open protocols POP, SMTP and IMAP; websites are still served up using the open protocol HTTP; bits are still circulated via the original open protocols of the internet, TCP/IP. You don't need to understand anything about how these software conventions work on a technical level to enjoy their benefits. The key characteristic they all share is that anyone can use them, free of charge. You don't need to pay a licensing fee to some corporation that owns HTTP if you want to put up a web page; you don't have to sell a part of your identity to advertisers if you want to send an email using SMTP. Along with Wikipedia, the open protocols of the internet constitute the most impressive example of commons-based production in human history.

To see how enormous but also invisible the benefits of such protocols have been, imagine that one of those key standards had not been developed: for instance, the open standard we use for defining our geographic location, GPS. Originally developed by the United States military, the Global Positioning System was first made available for civilian use during the Reagan administration. For about a decade, it was largely used by the aviation industry, until individual consumers began to use it in car navigation systems. And now we have smartphones that can pick up a signal from GPS satellites orbiting above us, and we use that extraordinary power to do everything from locating nearby restaurants to playing Pokémon Go to coordinating disaster-relief efforts.

But what if the military had kept GPS out of the public domain? Presumably, sometime in the 1990s, a market signal would have gone out to the innovators of Silicon Valley and other tech hubs, suggesting that consumers were interested in establishing their exact geographic coordinates so that those locations could be projected onto digital maps. There would have been a few years of furious competition among rival companies, who would toss their own proprietary satellites into orbit and advance their own unique protocols, but eventually the market would have settled on one dominant model, given all the efficiencies that result from a single, common way of verifying location. Call that imaginary firm GeoBook. Initially, the embrace of GeoBook would have been a leap forward for consumers and other companies trying to build location awareness into their hardware and software. But slowly, a darker narrative would have emerged: a single private corporation, tracking the movements of billions of people around the planet, building an advertising behemoth based on our shifting locations. Any start-up trying to build a geo-aware application would have been vulnerable to the whims of mighty GeoBook. Appropriately angry polemics would have been written denouncing the public menace of this Big Brother in the sky.

But none of that happened, for a simple reason. Geolocation, like the location of web pages and email addresses and domain names, is a problem we solved with an open protocol. And because it's a problem we don't have, we rarely think about how beautifully GPS does work and how many different applications have been built on its foundation.

The open, decentralized web turns out to be alive and well on the InternetOne layer. But since we settled on the World Wide Web in the mid-'90s, we've adopted very few new open-standard protocols. The biggest problems that technologists tackled after 1995 — many of which revolved around identity, community and payment mechanisms — were left to the private sector to solve. This is what led, in the early 2000s, to a powerful new layer of internet services, which we might call InternetTwo.

For all their brilliance, the inventors of the open protocols that shaped the internet failed to include some key elements that would later prove critical to the future of online culture. Perhaps most important, they did not create a secure open standard that established human identity on the network. Units of information could be defined — pages, links, messages — but *people* did not have their own protocol: no way to define and share your real name, your location, your interests or (perhaps most crucial) your relationships to other people online.

This turns out to have been a major oversight, because identity is the sort of problem that benefits from one universally recognized solution. It's what Vitalik Buterin, a founder of Ethereum, describes as "base-layer" infrastructure: things like language, roads and postal services, platforms where commerce and competition are actually assisted by having an underlying layer in the public domain. Offline, we don't have an open market for physical passports or Social Security numbers; we have a few reputable authorities — most of them backed by the power of the state — that we use to confirm to others that we are who we say we are. But online, the private sector swooped in to fill that vacuum, and because identity had that characteristic of being a universal problem, the market was heavily incentivized to settle on one common standard for defining yourself and the people you know.

The self-reinforcing feedback loops that economists call "increasing returns" or "network effects" kicked in, and after a period of experimentation in which we dabbled in social-media start-ups like Myspace and Friendster, the market settled on what is essentially a proprietary standard for establishing who you are and whom you know. That standard is Facebook. With more than two billion users, Facebook is far larger than the entire internet at the peak of the dot-com bubble in the late 1990s. And that user growth has made it the world's sixth-most-valuable corporation, just 14 years after it was founded. Facebook is the ultimate embodiment of the chasm that divides InternetOne and InternetTwo economies. No private company owned the protocols that defined email or GPS or the open web. But one single corporation owns the data that define social identity for two billion people today — and one single person, Mark Zuckerberg, holds the majority of the voting power in that corporation.

If you see the rise of the centralized web as an inevitable turn of the Cycle, and the open-protocol idealism of the early web as a kind of adolescent false consciousness, then there's less reason to fret about all the ways we've abandoned the vision of InternetOne. Either we're living in a fallen state today and there's no way to get back to Eden, or Eden itself was a kind of fantasy that was always going to be corrupted by concentrated power. In either case, there's no point in trying to restore the architecture of InternetOne; our only hope is to use the power of the state to rein in these corporate giants, through regulation and antitrust action. It's a variation of the old Audre Lorde maxim: "The master's tools will never dismantle the master's house." You can't fix the problems technology has created for us by throwing more technological solutions at it. You need forces outside the domain of software and servers to break up cartels with this much power.

But the thing about the master's house, in this analogy, is that it's a duplex. The upper floor has indeed been built with tools that cannot be used to dismantle it. But the open protocols beneath them still have the potential to build something better.

ONE OF THE MOST persuasive advocates of an open-protocol revival is Juan Benet, a Mexican-born programmer now living on a suburban side street in Palo Alto, Calif., in a three-bedroom rental that he shares with his girlfriend and another programmer, plus a rotating cast of guests, some of whom belong to Benet's organization, Protocol Labs. On a warm day in September, Benet greeted me at his door wearing a black Protocol Labs hoodie. The interior of the space brought to mind the incubator/frat house of HBO's "Silicon Valley," its living room commandeered by an array of black computer monitors. In the entrance hallway, the words "Welcome to Rivendell" were scrawled out on a whiteboard, a nod to the Elven city from "Lord of the Rings." "We call this house Rivendell," Benet said sheepishly. "It's not a very good Rivendell. It doesn't have enough books, or waterfalls, or elves."

Benet, who is 29, considers himself a child of the first peer-to-peer revolution that briefly flourished in the late 1990s and early 2000s, driven in large part by networks like BitTorrent that distributed media files, often illegally. That initial flowering was in many ways a logical outgrowth of the internet's decentralized, open-protocol roots. The web had shown that you could publish documents reliably in a commons-based network. Services like BitTorrent or Skype took that logic to the next level, allowing ordinary users to add new functionality to the internet: creating a distributed library of (largely pirated) media, as with BitTorrent, or helping people make phone calls over the internet, as with Skype.

Sitting in the living room/office at Rivendell, Benet told me that he thinks of the early 2000s, with the ascent of Skype and BitTorrent, as "the 'summer' of peer-to-peer" — its salad days. "But then peer-to-peer hit a wall, because people started to prefer centralized architectures," he said. "And partly because the peer-to-peer business models were piracy-driven." A graduate of Stanford's computer-science program, Benet talks in a manner reminiscent of Elon Musk: As he speaks, his eyes dart across an empty space above your head, almost as though he's reading an invisible teleprompter to find the words. He is passionate about the technology Protocol Labs is developing, but also keen to put it in a wider context. For Benet, the shift from distributed systems to more centralized approaches set in motion changes that few could have predicted. "The rules of the game, the rules that govern all of this technology, matter a lot," he said. "The structure of what we build now will paint a very different picture of the way things will be five or 10 years in the future." He continued: "It was clear to me then that peer-to-peer was this extraordinary thing. What was not clear to me then was how at risk it is. It was not clear to me that you had to take up the baton, that it's now your turn to protect it."

Protocol Labs is Benet's attempt to take up that baton, and its first project is a radical overhaul of the internet's file system, including the basic scheme we use to address the location of pages on the web. Benet calls his system IPFS, short for InterPlanetary File System. The current protocol — HTTP — pulls down web pages from a single location at a time and has no built-in mechanism for archiving the online pages. IPFS allows users to download a page simultaneously from multiple locations and includes what programmers call "historic versioning," so that past iterations do not vanish from the historical record. To support the protocol, Benet is also creating a system called Filecoin that will allow users to effectively rent out unused hard-drive space. (Think of it as a sort of Airbnb for data.) "Right now there are tons of hard drives around the planet that are doing nothing, or close to nothing, to the point where their owners are just losing money," Benet said. "So you can bring online a massive amount of supply, which will bring down the costs of storage." But as its name suggests, Protocol Labs has an ambition that extends beyond these projects; Benet's larger mission is to support many new open-source protocols in the years to come.

Why did the internet follow the path from open to closed? One part of the explanation lies in sins of omission: By the time a new generation of coders began to tackle the problems that InternetOne left unsolved, there were near-limitless sources of capital to invest in those efforts, so long as the coders kept their systems closed. The secret to the success of the open protocols of InternetOne is that they were developed in an age when most people didn't care about online networks, so they were able to stealthily reach critical mass without having to contend with wealthy conglomerates and venture capitalists. By the mid-2000s, though, a promising new start-up like Facebook could attract millions of dollars in financing even before it became a household brand. And that private-sector money ensured that the company's key software would remain closed, in order to capture as much value as possible for shareholders.

And yet — as the venture capitalist Chris Dixon points out — there was another factor, too, one that was more technical than financial in nature. "Let's say you're trying to build an open Twitter," Dixon explained while sitting in a conference room at the New York offices of Andreessen Horowitz, where he is a general partner. "I'm @cdixon at Twitter. Where do you store that? You need a database." A closed architecture like Facebook's or Twitter's puts all the information about its users — their handles, their likes and photos, the map of connections they have to other individuals on the network — into a private database that is maintained by the company. Whenever you look at your Facebook newsfeed, you are granted access to some infinitesimally small section of that database, seeing only the information that is relevant to you.

Running Facebook's database is an unimaginably complex operation, relying on hundreds of thousands of servers scattered around the world, overseen by some of the most brilliant engineers on the planet. From Facebook's point of view, they're providing a valuable service to humanity: creating a common social graph for almost everyone on earth. The fact that they have to sell ads to pay the bills for that service — and the fact that the scale of their network gives them staggering power over the minds of two billion people around the world — is an unfortunate, but inevitable, price to pay for a shared social graph. And that trade-off did in fact make sense in the mid-2000s; creating a single database capable of tracking the interactions of hundreds of millions of people — much less two billion — was the kind of problem that could be tackled only by a single organization. But as Benet and his fellow blockchain evangelists are eager to prove, that might not be true anymore.

So how can you get meaningful adoption of base-layer protocols in an age when the big tech companies have already attracted billions of users and collectively sit on hundreds of billions of dollars in cash? If you happen to believe that the internet, in its current incarnation, is causing significant and growing harm to society, then this seemingly esoteric problem — the difficulty of getting people to adopt new open-source technology standards — turns out to have momentous consequences. If we can't figure out a way to introduce new, rival base-layer infrastructure, then we're stuck with the internet we have today. The best we can hope for is government interventions to scale back the power of Facebook or Google, or some kind of consumer revolt that encourages that marketplace to shift to less hegemonic online services, the digital equivalent of forswearing big agriculture for local farmers' markets. Neither approach would upend the underlying dynamics of InternetTwo.

THE FIRST HINT of a meaningful challenge to the closed-protocol era arrived in 2008, not long after Zuckerberg opened the first international headquarters for his growing company. A mysterious programmer (or group of programmers) going by the name Satoshi Nakamoto circulated a paper on a cryptography mailing list. The paper was called "Bitcoin: A Peer-to-Peer Electronic Cash System," and in it, Nakamoto outlined an ingenious system for a digital currency that did not require a centralized trusted authority to verify transactions. At the time, Facebook and Bitcoin seemed to belong to entirely different spheres — one was a booming venture-backed social-media start-up that let you share birthday greetings and connect with old friends, while the other was a byzantine scheme for cryptographic currency from an obscure email list. But 10 years later, the ideas that Nakamoto unleashed with that paper now pose the most significant challenge to the hegemony of InternetTwo giants like Facebook.

The paradox about Bitcoin is that it may well turn out to be a genuinely revolutionary breakthrough and at the same time a colossal failure as a currency. As I write, Bitcoin has increased in value by nearly 100,000 percent over the past five years, making a fortune for its early investors but also branding it as a spectacularly unstable payment mechanism. The process for creating new Bitcoins has also turned out to be a staggering energy drain.

History is replete with stories of new technologies whose initial applications end up having little to do with their eventual use. All the focus on Bitcoin as a payment system may similarly prove to be a distraction, a technological red herring. Nakamoto pitched Bitcoin as a "peer-to-peer electronic-cash system" in the initial manifesto, but at its heart, the innovation he (or she or they) was proposing had a more general structure, with two key features.

First, Bitcoin offered a kind of proof that you could create a secure database — the blockchain — scattered across hundreds or thousands of computers, with no single authority controlling and verifying the authenticity of the data.

Second, Nakamoto designed Bitcoin so that the work of maintaining that distributed ledger was itself rewarded with small, increasingly scarce Bitcoin payments. If you dedicated half your computer's processing cycles to helping the Bitcoin network get its math right — and thus fend off the hackers and scam artists — you received a small sliver of the currency. Nakamoto designed the system so that Bitcoins would grow increasingly difficult to earn over time, ensuring a certain amount of scarcity in the system. If you helped Bitcoin keep that database secure in the early days, you would earn more Bitcoin than later arrivals. This process has come to be called "mining."

For our purposes, forget everything else about the Bitcoin frenzy, and just keep these two things in mind: What Nakamoto ushered into the world was a way of agreeing on the contents of a database without anyone being "in charge" of the database, and a way of compensating people for helping make that database more valuable, without those people being on an official payroll or owning shares in a corporate entity. Together, those two ideas solved the distributed-database problem and the funding problem. Suddenly there was a way of supporting open protocols that wasn't available during the infancy of Facebook and Twitter.

These two features have now been replicated in dozens of new systems inspired by Bitcoin. One of those systems is Ethereum, proposed in a white paper by Vitalik Buterin when he was just 19. Ethereum does have its currencies, but at its heart Ethereum was designed less to facilitate electronic payments than to allow people to run applications on top of the Ethereum blockchain. There are currently hundreds of Ethereum apps in development, ranging from prediction markets to Facebook clones to crowdfunding services. Almost all of them are in pre-alpha stage, not ready for consumer adoption. Despite the embryonic state of the applications, the Ether currency has seen its own miniature version of the Bitcoin bubble, most likely making Buterin an immense fortune.

These currencies can be used in clever ways. Juan Benet's Filecoin system will rely on Ethereum technology and reward users and developers who adopt its IPFS protocol or help maintain the shared database it requires. Protocol Labs is creating its own cryptocurrency, also called Filecoin, and has plans to sell some of those coins on the open market in the coming months. (In the summer of 2017, the company raised $135 million in the first 60 minutes of what Benet calls a "presale" of the tokens to accredited investors.) Many cryptocurrencies are first made available to the public through a process known as an initial coin offering, or I.C.O.

The I.C.O. abbreviation is a deliberate echo of the initial public offering that so defined the first internet bubble in the 1990s. But there is a crucial difference between the two. Speculators can buy in during an I.C.O., but they are not buying an ownership stake in a private company and its proprietary software, the way they might in a traditional I.P.O. Afterward, the coins will continue to be created in exchange for labor — in the case of Filecoin, by anyone who helps maintain the Filecoin network. Developers who help refine the software can earn the coins, as can ordinary users who lend out spare hard-drive space to expand the network's storage capacity. The Filecoin is a way of signaling that someone, somewhere, has added value to the network.

Advocates like Chris Dixon have started referring to the compensation side of the equation in terms of "tokens," not coins, to emphasize that the technology here isn't necessarily aiming to disrupt existing currency systems. "I like the metaphor of a token because it makes it very clear that it's like an arcade," he says. "You go to the arcade, and in the arcade you can use these tokens. But we're not trying to replace the U.S. government. It's not meant to be a real currency; it's meant to be a pseudo-currency inside this world." Dan Finlay, a creator of MetaMask, echoes Dixon's argument. "To me, what's interesting about this is that we get to program new value systems," he says. "They don't have to resemble money."

Pseudo or not, the idea of an I.C.O. has already inspired a host of shady offerings, some of them endorsed by celebrities who would seem to be unlikely blockchain enthusiasts, like DJ Khaled, Paris Hilton and Floyd Mayweather. In a blog post published in October 2017, Fred Wilson, a founder of Union Square Ventures and an early advocate of the blockchain revolution, thundered against the spread of I.C.O.s. "I hate it," Wilson wrote, adding that most I.C.O.s "are scams. And the celebrities and others who promote them on their social-media channels in an effort to enrich themselves are behaving badly and possibly violating securities laws." Arguably the most striking thing about the surge of interest in I.C.O.s — and in existing currencies like Bitcoin or Ether — is how much financial speculation has already gravitated to platforms that have effectively zero adoption among ordinary consumers. At least during the internet bubble of late 1990s, ordinary people were buying books on Amazon or reading newspapers online; there was clear evidence that the web was going to become a mainstream platform. Today, the hype cycles are so accelerated that billions of dollars are chasing a technology that almost no one outside the cryptocommunity understands, much less uses.

LET'S SAY, for the sake of argument, that the hype is warranted, and blockchain platforms like Ethereum become a fundamental part of our digital infrastructure. How would a distributed ledger and a token economy somehow challenge one of the tech giants? One of Fred Wilson's partners at Union Square Ventures, Brad Burnham, suggests a scenario revolving around another tech giant that has run afoul of regulators and public opinion in the last year: Uber. "Uber is basically just a coordination platform between drivers and passengers," Burnham says. "Yes, it was really innovative, and there were a bunch of things in the beginning about reducing the anxiety of whether the driver was coming or not, and the map — and a whole bunch of things that you should give them a lot of credit for." But when a new service like Uber starts to take off, there's a strong incentive for the marketplace to consolidate around a single leader. The fact that more passengers are starting to use the Uber app attracts more drivers to the service, which in turn attracts more passengers. People have their credit cards stored with Uber; they have the app installed already; there are far more Uber drivers on the road. And so the switching costs of trying out some other rival service eventually become prohibitive, even if the chief executive seems to be a jerk or if consumers would, in the abstract, prefer a competitive marketplace with a dozen Ubers. "At some point, the innovation around the coordination becomes less and less innovative," Burnham says.

The blockchain world proposes something different. Imagine some group like Protocol Labs decides there's a case to be made for adding another "basic layer" to the stack. Just as GPS gave us a way of discovering and sharing our location, this new protocol would define a simple request: I am here and would like to go there. A distributed ledger might record all its users' past trips, credit cards, favorite locations — all the metadata that services like Uber or Amazon use to encourage lock-in.

Call it, for the sake of argument, the Transit protocol. The standards for sending a Transit request out onto the internet would be entirely open; anyone who wanted to build an app to respond to that request would be free to do so. Cities could build Transit apps that allowed taxi drivers to field requests. But so could bike-share collectives, or rickshaw drivers. Developers could create shared marketplace apps where all the potential vehicles using Transit could vie for your business. When you walked out on the sidewalk and tried to get a ride, you wouldn't have to place your allegiance with a single provider before hailing. You would simply announce that you were standing at 67th and Madison and needed to get to Union Square. And then you'd get a flurry of competing offers. You could even theoretically get an offer from the M.T.A., which could build a service to remind Transit users that it might be much cheaper and faster just to jump on the 6 train.

How would Transit reach critical mass when Uber and Lyft already dominate the ride-sharing market? This is where the tokens come in. Early adopters of Transit would be rewarded with Transit tokens, which could themselves be used to purchase Transit services or be traded on exchanges for traditional currency. As in the Bitcoin model, tokens would be doled out less generously as Transit grew more popular. In the early days, a developer who built an iPhone app that uses Transit might see a windfall of tokens; Uber drivers who started using Transit as a second option for finding passengers could collect tokens as a reward for embracing the system; adventurous consumers would be rewarded with tokens for using Transit in its early days, when there are fewer drivers available compared with the existing proprietary networks like Uber or Lyft.

As Transit began to take off, it would attract speculators, who would put a monetary price on the token and drive even more interest in the protocol by inflating its value, which in turn would attract more developers, drivers and customers. If the whole system ends up working as its advocates believe, the result is a more competitive but at the same time more equitable marketplace. Instead of all the economic value being captured by the shareholders of one or two large corporations that dominate the market, the economic value is distributed across a much wider group: the early developers of Transit, the app creators who make the protocol work in a consumer-friendly form, the early-adopter drivers and passengers, the first wave of speculators. Token economies introduce a strange new set of elements that do not fit the traditional models: instead of creating value by owning something, as in the shareholder equity model, people create value by improving the underlying protocol, either by helping to maintain the ledger (as in Bitcoin mining), or by writing apps atop it, or simply by using the service. The lines between founders, investors and customers are far blurrier than in traditional corporate models; all the incentives are explicitly designed to steer away from winner-take-all outcomes. And yet at the same time, the whole system depends on an initial speculative phase in which outsiders are betting on the token to rise in value.

"You think about the '90s internet bubble and all the great infrastructure we got out of that," Dixon says. "You're basically taking that effect and shrinking it down to the size of an application."

EVEN DECENTRALIZED CRYPTOMOVEMENTS have their key nodes. For Ethereum, one of those nodes is the Brooklyn headquarters of an organization called ConsenSys, founded by Joseph Lubin, an early Ethereum pioneer. In November, Amanda Gutterman, the 26-year-old chief marketing officer for ConsenSys, gave me a tour of the space. In our first few minutes together, she offered the obligatory cup of coffee, only to discover that the drip-coffee machine in the kitchen was bone dry. "How can we fix the internet if we can't even make coffee?" she said with a laugh.

Planted in industrial Bushwick, a stone's throw from the pizza mecca Roberta's, "headquarters" seemed an unlikely word. The front door was festooned with graffiti and stickers; inside, the stairwells of the space appeared to have been last renovated during the Coolidge administration. Just about three years old, the ConsenSys network now includes more than 550 employees in 28 countries, and the operation has never raised a dime of venture capital. As an organization, ConsenSys does not quite fit any of the usual categories: It is technically a corporation, but it has elements that also resemble nonprofits and workers' collectives. The shared goal of ConsenSys members is strengthening and expanding the Ethereum blockchain. They support developers creating new apps and tools for the platform, one of which is MetaMask, the software that generated my Ethereum address. But they also offer consulting-style services for companies, nonprofits or governments looking for ways to integrate Ethereum's smart contracts into their own systems.

The true test of the blockchain will revolve — like so many of the online crises of the past few years — around the problem of identity. Today your digital identity is scattered across dozens, or even hundreds, of different sites: Amazon has your credit-card information and your purchase history; Facebook knows your friends and family; Equifax maintains your credit history. When you use any of those services, you are effectively asking for permission to borrow some of that information about yourself in order perform a task: ordering a Christmas present for your uncle, checking Instagram to see pictures from the office party last night. But all these different fragments of your identity don't belong to you; they belong to Facebook and Amazon and Google, who are free to sell bits of that information about you to advertisers without consulting you. You, of course, are free to delete those accounts if you choose, and if you stop checking Facebook, Zuckerberg and the Facebook shareholders will stop making money by renting out your attention to their true customers. But your Facebook or Google identity isn't portable. If you want to join another promising social network that is maybe a little less infected with Russian bots, you can't extract your social network from Twitter and deposit it in the new service. You have to build the network again from scratch (and persuade all your friends to do the same).

The blockchain evangelists think this entire approach is backward. You should own your digital identity — which could include everything from your date of birth to your friend networks to your purchasing history — and you should be free to lend parts of that identity out to services as you see fit. Given that identity was not baked into the original internet protocols, and given the difficulty of managing a distributed database in the days before Bitcoin, this form of "self-sovereign" identity — as the parlance has it — was a practical impossibility. Now it is an attainable goal. A number of blockchain-based services are trying to tackle this problem, including a new identity system called uPort that has been spun out of ConsenSys and another one called Blockstack that is currently based on the Bitcoin platform. (Tim Berners-Lee is leading the development of a comparable system, called Solid, that would also give users control over their own data.) These rival protocols all have slightly different frameworks, but they all share a general vision of how identity should work on a truly decentralized internet.

What would prevent a new blockchain-based identity standard from following Tim Wu's Cycle, the same one that brought Facebook to such a dominant position? Perhaps nothing. But imagine how that sequence would play out in practice. Someone creates a new protocol to define your social network via Ethereum. It might be as simple as a list of other Ethereum addresses; in other words, *Here are the public addresses of people I like and trust.* That way of defining your social network might well take off and ultimately supplant the closed systems that define your network on Facebook. Perhaps someday, every single person on the planet might use that standard to map their social connections, just as every single person on the internet uses TCP/IP to share data. But even if this new form of identity became ubiquitous, it wouldn't present the same opportunities for abuse and manipulation that you find in the closed systems that have become de facto standards. I might allow a Facebook-style service to use my social map to filter news or gossip or music for me, based on the activity of my friends, but if that service annoyed me, I'd be free to sample other alternatives without the switching costs. An open identity standard would give ordinary people the opportunity to sell their attention to the highest bidder, or choose to keep it out of the marketplace altogether.

Gutterman suggests that the same kind of system could be applied to even more critical forms of identity, like health care data. Instead of storing, say, your genome on servers belonging to a private corporation, the information would instead be stored inside a personal data archive. "There may be many corporate entities that I don't want seeing that data, but maybe I'd like to donate that data to a medical study," she says. "I could use my blockchain-based self-sovereign ID to [allow] one group to use it and not another. Or I could sell it over here and give it away over there."

The token architecture would give a blockchain-based identity standard an additional edge over closed standards like Facebook's. As many critics have observed, ordinary users on social-media platforms create almost all the content without compensation, while the companies capture all the economic value from that content through advertising sales. A token-based social network would at least give early adopters a piece of the action, rewarding them for their labors in making the new platform appealing. "If someone can really figure out a version of Facebook that lets users own a piece of the network and get paid," Dixon says, "that could be pretty compelling."

Would that information be more secure in a distributed blockchain than behind the elaborate firewalls of giant corporations like Google or Facebook? In this one respect, the Bitcoin story is actually instructive: It may never be stable enough to function as a currency, but it does offer convincing proof of just how secure a distributed ledger can be. "Look at the market cap of Bitcoin or Ethereum: $80 billion, $25 billion, whatever," Dixon says. "That means if you successfully attack that system, you could walk away with more than a billion dollars. You know what a 'bug bounty' is? Someone says, 'If you hack my system, I'll give you a million dollars.' So Bitcoin is now a nine-year-old multibillion-dollar bug bounty, and no one's hacked it. It feels like pretty good proof."

Additional security would come from the decentralized nature of these new identity protocols. In the identity system proposed by Blockstack, the actual information about your identity — your social connections, your purchasing history — could be stored anywhere online. The blockchain would simply provide cryptographically secure keys to unlock that information and share it with other trusted providers. A system with a centralized repository with data for hundreds of millions of users — what security experts call "honey pots" — is far more appealing to hackers. Which would you rather do: steal a hundred million credit histories by hacking into a hundred million separate personal computers and sniffing around until you found the right data on each machine? Or just hack into one honey pot at Equifax and walk away with the same amount of data in a matter of hours? As Gutterman puts it, "It's the difference between robbing a house versus robbing the entire village."

SO MUCH OF the blockchain's architecture is shaped by predictions about how that architecture might be abused once it finds a wider audience. That is part of its charm and its power. The blockchain channels the energy of speculative bubbles by allowing tokens to be shared widely among true supporters of the platform. It safeguards against any individual or small group gaining control of the entire database. Its cryptography is designed to protect against surveillance states or identity thieves. In this, the blockchain displays a familial resemblance to political constitutions: Its rules are designed with one eye on how those rules might be exploited down the line.

Much has been made of the anarcho-libertarian streak in Bitcoin and other nonfiat currencies; the community is rife with words and phrases ("self-sovereign") that sound as if they could be slogans for some militia compound in Montana. And yet in its potential to break up large concentrations of power and explore less-proprietary models of ownership, the blockchain idea offers a tantalizing possibility for those who would like to distribute wealth more equitably and break up the cartels of the digital age.

The blockchain worldview can also sound libertarian in the sense that it proposes nonstate solutions to capitalist excesses like information monopolies. But to believe in the blockchain is not necessarily to oppose regulation, if that regulation is designed with complementary aims. Brad Burnham, for instance, suggests that regulators should insist that everyone have "a right to a private data store," where all the various facets of their online identity would be maintained. But governments wouldn't be required to design those identity protocols. They would be developed on the blockchain, open source. Ideologically speaking, that private data store would be a true team effort: built as an intellectual commons, funded by token speculators, supported by the regulatory state.

Like the original internet itself, the blockchain is an idea with radical — almost communitarian — possibilities that at the same time has attracted some of the most frivolous and regressive appetites of capitalism. We spent our first years online in a world defined by open protocols and intellectual commons; we spent the second phase in a world increasingly dominated by closed architectures and proprietary databases. We have learned enough from this history to support the hypothesis that open works better than closed, at least where base-layer issues are concerned. But we don't have an easy route back to the open-protocol era. Some messianic next-generation internet protocol is not likely to emerge out of Department of Defense research, the way the first-generation internet did nearly 50 years ago.

Yes, the blockchain may seem like the very worst of speculative capitalism right now, and yes, it is demonically challenging to understand. But the beautiful thing about open protocols is that they can be steered in surprising new directions by the people who discover and champion them in their infancy. Right now, the only real hope for a revival of the open-protocol ethos lies in the blockchain. Whether it eventually lives up to its egalitarian promise will in large part depend on the people who embrace the platform, who take up the baton, as

Juan Benet puts it, from those early online pioneers. If you think the internet is not working in its current incarnation, you can't change the system through think-pieces and F.C.C. regulations alone. You need new code.

STEVEN JOHNSON is the author of 10 books, most recently "Wonderland." He last wrote for the magazine about the science of communicating with extraterrestrials.

Making a Crypto Utopia in Puerto Rico

BY NELLIE BOWLES | FEB. 2, 2018

SAN JUAN, P.R. — They call what they are building Puertopia. But then someone told them, apparently in all seriousness, that it translates to "eternal boy playground" in Latin. So they are changing the name: They will call it Sol.

Dozens of entrepreneurs, made newly wealthy by blockchain and cryptocurrencies, are heading en masse to Puerto Rico this winter. They are selling their homes and cars in California and establishing residency on the Caribbean island in hopes of avoiding what they see as onerous state and federal taxes on their growing fortunes, some of which now reach into the billions of dollars.

And these men — because they are almost exclusively men — have a plan for what to do with the wealth: They want to build a crypto utopia, a new city where the money is virtual and the contracts are all public, to show the rest of the world what a crypto future could look like. Blockchain, a digital ledger that forms the basis of virtual currencies, has the potential to reinvent society — and the Puertopians want to prove it.

For more than a year, the entrepreneurs had been searching for the best location. After Hurricane Maria decimated Puerto Rico's infrastructure in September and the price of cryptocurrencies began to soar, they saw an opportunity and felt a sense of urgency.

So this crypto community flocked here to create its paradise. Now the investors are spending their days hunting for property where they could have their own airports and docks. They are taking over hotels and a museum in the capital's historic section, called Old San Juan. They say they are close to getting the local government to allow them to have the first cryptocurrency bank.

"What's happened here is a perfect storm," said Halsey Minor, the founder of the news site CNET, who is moving his new blockchain company — called Videocoin — from the Cayman Islands to Puerto Rico this winter. Referring to Hurricane Maria and the investment interest that has followed, he added, "While it was really bad for the people of Puerto Rico, in the long term it's a godsend if people look past that."

Puerto Rico offers an unparalleled tax incentive: no federal personal income taxes, no capital gains tax and favorable business taxes — all without having to renounce your American citizenship. For now, the local government seems receptive toward the crypto utopians; the governor will speak at their blockchain summit conference, called Puerto Crypto, in March.

The territory's go-to blockchain tax lawyer is Giovanni Mendez, 30. He expected the tax expatriates to disappear after Hurricane Maria, but the population has instead boomed.

"It's increased monumentally," said Mr. Mendez, who has about two dozen crypto clients. "And they all came together."

The movement is alarming an earlier generation of Puerto Rico tax expats like the hedge fund manager Robb Rill, who runs a social group for those taking advantage of the tax incentives.

"They call me up saying they're going to buy 250,000 acres so they can incorporate their own city, literally start a city in Puerto Rico to have their own crypto world," said Mr. Rill, who moved to the island in 2013. "I can't engage in that."

The newcomers are still debating the exact shape that Puertopia should take. Some think they need to make a city; others think it's enough to move into Old San Juan. Puertopians said, however, that they hoped to move very fast.

"You've never seen an industry catalyze a place like you're going to see here," Mr. Minor said.

THE MONASTERY

Until the Puertopians find land, they have descended on the Monastery, a 20,000-square-foot hotel they rented as their base and that was largely unscathed by the hurricane.

Brock Pierce, center, with Josh Boles, left, and Matt Clemenson on the roof of the Monastery, a San Juan hotel that has been rented out as the entrepreneurs' temporary headquarters.

Matt Clemenson and Stephen Morris were drinking beer on the Monastery's roof one recent evening. Mr. Clemenson had an easygoing affect and wore two-tone aviators; Mr. Morris, a loquacious British man, was in cargo shorts and lace-up steel-toed combat boots, with a smartphone on a necklace. They wanted to make two things clear: They chose Puerto Rico because of the hurricane, and they come in peace.

"It's only when everything's been swept away that you can make a case for rebuilding from the ground up," Mr. Morris, 53, said.

"We're benevolent capitalists, building a benevolent economy," said Mr. Clemenson, 34, a co-founder of Lottery.com, which is using the blockchain in lotteries. "Puerto Rico has been this hidden gem, this enchanted island that's been consistently overlooked and mistreated. Maybe 500 years later we can make it right."

Other Puertopians arrived on the roof as a pack, just back from a full-day property-hunting bus tour. From the middle, Brock Pierce, 37, the leader of the Puertopia movement, emerged wearing drop crotch capri pants, a black vest that almost hit his knees and a large black felt hat. He and others had arrived on the island in early December.

"Compassion, respect, financial transparency," Mr. Pierce said when asked what was guiding them here.

Mr. Pierce, the director of the Bitcoin Foundation, is a major figure in the crypto boom. He co-founded a blockchain-for-business start-up, Block.One, which has sold around $200 million of a custom virtual currency, EOS, in a so-called initial coin offering. The value of all the outstanding EOS tokens is around $6.5 billion.

A former child actor, Mr. Pierce got into digital money early as a professional gamer, mining and trading gold in the video game World of Warcraft, an effort funded partly by Stephen K. Bannon, the former Trump adviser. Mr. Pierce is a controversial figure — he has previously been sued for fraud, among other matters.

Downstairs, in the Monastery penthouse, a dozen or so other expats were hanging out. The water was out that night, so the toilets and faucets were dry. Mr. Minor lounged on an alcove chaise.

"The U.S. doesn't want us. It's trying to choke off this economy," Mr. Minor said, referring to the difficulties that crypto investors have with American banks. "There needs to be a place where people are free to invent."

Mr. Pierce paced the room with his hands in fists. A few times a day, he played a video for the group on his phone and a portable speaker: Charlie Chaplin's 1940 "The Great Dictator," in which Chaplin parodies Hitler rallying his forces. He finds inspiration in lines like "More than machinery, we need humanity."

"I'm worried people are going to misinterpret our actions," Mr. Pierce said. "That we're just coming to Puerto Rico to dodge taxes."

He said he was aiming to create a charitable token called ONE with $1 billion of his own money. "If you take the MY out of money, you're left with ONE," Mr. Pierce said.

"He's tuned in to a higher calling," said Kai Nygard, scion of the

Canadian clothing company Nygard and a crypto investor. "He's beyond money."

The force of Mr. Pierce's personality and his spiritual presence are important to the group, whose members are otherwise largely agnostic. Mr. Pierce regularly performs rituals. Earlier that day while scoping out property, they had stopped at a historic Ceiba tree, known as the Tree of Life.

"Brock nestled into the bosom of it and was there for 10 minutes," Mr. Nygard said.

Mr. Pierce walked around the tree and said prayers for Puertopia, holding a rusted wrench he had picked up in the territory. He kissed an old man's feet. He blessed a crystal in the water, as they all watched. He played the Chaplin speech to everyone and to the tree, Mr. Nygard said.

That wrench is now in the penthouse, heavy and greasy.

Later on, at a dinner in a nearby restaurant, the group ordered platters of octopus arms, fried cheese, ceviche and rum cocktails. They began debating whether to buy Puerto Rico's Roosevelt Roads Naval Station, which measures 9,000 acres and has two deepwater ports and an adjacent airport. The only hitch: It's a Superfund cleanup site.

Mr. Pierce had fallen asleep by then, his hat tilted down and arms crossed. He gets two hours of sleep many nights, often on a firm grounding mat to stay in contact with the earth's electric energy. Josh Boles, a tall, athletic man who is another crypto expat, picked him up, and the group headed back to the Monastery.

They walked past a big pink building in an old town square, the start of their vision for Puertopia's downtown. Once a children's museum, they plan on making it a crypto clubhouse and outreach center that will have the mission "to bring together Puerto Ricans with Puertopians."

THE VANDERBILT

Workdays are casual in Puertopia. One morning, Bryan Larkin, 39, and Reeve Collins, 42, were working at another old hotel, the Condado

Mr. Pierce and Mr. Boles sitting with Robert Anderson, right, at the Monastery, which was left largely unscathed by Hurricane Maria in 2017.

Vanderbilt, where they had their laptops on a pool bar with frozen piña coladas on tap.

"We're going to make this crypto land," Mr. Larkin said.

Mr. Larkin has mined about $2 billion in Bitcoin and is the chief technology officer of Blockchain Industries, a publicly traded company based in Puerto Rico.

Mr. Collins, an internet veteran, had raised more than $20 million from an initial coin offering for BlockV, his app store for the blockchain, whose outstanding tokens are worth about $125 million. He had also co-founded Tether, which backs cryptocurrency tied to the value of a dollar and whose outstanding tokens are worth about $2.1 billion, though the company has generated enormous controversy in the virtual currency world.

"So, no. No, I don't want to pay taxes," Mr. Collins said. "This is the first time in human history anyone other than kings or governments or gods can create their own money."

He had moved from Santa Monica, Calif., with just a few bags and was now starting a local cryptocurrency incubator called Vatom Factory.

"When Brock said, 'We're moving to Puerto Rico for the taxes and to create this new town,' I said, 'I'm in,'" Mr. Collins said. "Sight unseen."

They soon went back to work, checking out Coinmarketcap.com, a site that shows the price of cryptocurrencies.

"Our market cap's gone up $100 million in a week," Mr. Collins said.

"Congrats, man," Mr. Larkin said.

WELCOME, PUERTOPIANS?

All across San Juan, many locals are trying to figure out what to do with the crypto arrivals.

Some are open to the new wave as a welcome infusion of investment and ideas.

"We're open for crypto business," said Erika Medina-Vecchini, the chief business development officer for the Department of Economic Development and Commerce, in an interview at her office. She said her office was starting an ad campaign aimed at the new crypto expat boom, with the tagline "Paradise Performs."

Others worry about the island's being used for an experiment and talk about "crypto colonialism." At a house party in San Juan, Richard Lopez, 32, who runs a pizza restaurant, Estella, in the town of Arecibo, said: "I think it's great. Lure them in with taxes, and they'll spend money."

Andria Satz, 33, who grew up in Old San Juan and works for the Conservation Trust of Puerto Rico, disagreed.

"We're the tax playground for the rich," she said. "We're the test case for anyone who wants to experiment. Outsiders get tax exemptions, and locals can't get permits."

Mr. Lopez said the territory needed something to jump-start the economy. "We have to find a new way," he said.

"Sure then, Bitcoin, why not," Ms. Satz said, throwing up her hands.

Mr. Lopez said he and a childhood friend, Rafael Perez, 31, were trying to set up a Bitcoin mine in their hometown. But electricity has been inconsistent, and mining even a single Bitcoin takes a lot of power, he said.

Have a Cryptocurrency Company? Bermuda, Malta or Gibraltar Wants You

BY NATHANIEL POPPER | JULY 29, 2018

SAN FRANCISCO — Hedge funds go to the Cayman Islands to incorporate. Big companies are generally domiciled in Delaware. And online poker companies often set up their bases in Gibraltar and Malta.

Now the race is on to become the go-to destination for cryptocurrency companies that are looking for shelter from regulatory uncertainty in the United States and Asia.

In small countries and territories including Bermuda, Malta, Gibraltar and Liechtenstein, officials have recently passed laws, or have legislation in the works, to make themselves more welcoming to cryptocurrency companies and projects. In Malta, the government passed three laws on July 4 so companies can easily issue new cryptocurrencies and trade existing ones. In Bermuda this year, the legislature passed a law that lets start-ups doing initial coin offerings apply to the minister of finance for speedy approval.

"We are 65,000 people, and 20 square miles, but we have a very advanced economy," the premier of Bermuda, E. David Burt, said in an interview at a cryptocurrency conference in May in New York, where he was trying to pitch companies on the island's charms. "We want to position Bermuda as the incubator for this industry."

The competition for cryptocurrency companies is part of a broader rush by governments to figure out how to approach a new industry that took on outsize prominence over the last year. Becoming a crypto center has many potential upsides, including jobs and tax revenue.

But the drive to be a crypto nexus also comes with significant risk. Hackings and scams have followed the industry everywhere it has gone. They have been aided by the underlying technology introduced by Bitcoin, known as the blockchain, which was built to make it possible to send money without requiring approval from government agencies or existing financial institutions. And the cryptocurrencies are hardly stable, with the prices of most having plunged in 2018 after skyrocketing last year.

The use of cryptocurrencies by hackers was reinforced this month when the Justice Department announced charges against 12 Russian intelligence officers accused of hacking the Democratic National Committee and said they had principally used Bitcoin to fund their work.

Volatility and uncertainty have deterred some countries and caused others to hesitate in embracing crypto companies. In China, the government banned cryptocurrency exchanges and initial coin offerings after many of its citizens were swept up in the frenzy and bet their savings on digital tokens. And the Japanese authorities halted the operations of several crypto exchanges this year after one of the biggest licensed exchanges was hacked.

In the United States, the head of the Securities and Exchange Commission, Jay Clayton, has warned that most companies that have raised money by selling cryptocurrencies have most likely not followed the law. But his agency has not provided clear guidance on the line demarcating legal and illegal projects.

All of this has opened the door for smaller countries to provide a friendlier environment, separate from private efforts — such as in Puerto Rico — to create crypto havens. And many of the countries' moves are already having an effect, with dozens of companies — including the largest exchange in the world — announcing plans to set up offices in the small jurisdictions that have passed laws.

Bermuda has been a leading player. Apart from passing the law to allow for fast approval of initial coin offerings, the British territory has a law in the works to open the doors to cryptocurrency exchanges and related services. Mr. Burt said his government was modeling its approach on one it had taken with the insurance industry, in which Bermuda has become a major player.

In Malta, the government passed three laws on July 4 so companies can easily issue new cryptocurrencies and trade existing ones.

Bermuda's measures have attracted Will McDonough, the founder of a new cryptocurrency called iCash. He said he had decided to base his company there because of the island's experience in international finance and the government's willingness to listen to the company's input.

"The largest issue blockchain companies have is not knowing how they'll be governed or regulated," said Mr. McDonough, a former vice president at Goldman Sachs. "Those markets that have made the rules clear have found many companies coming to play by the rules."

Mr. McDonough is planning to raise $35 million by selling iCash tokens to investors around the world, including some in the United States. The iCash tokens are initially designed to be the method of payment for an online gambling site. He said he would still be based in Florida, but would have an office and a head of operations in Bermuda, which the island requires of all companies.

Other companies are playing the field more. Binance, the world's largest cryptocurrency exchange, went shopping for a new location after Japan shut it down this year for operating without a license. The exchange, which is known for its desire to skirt regulations, announced in March that it would open new offices in Malta with hundreds of employees as a result of the friendly laws the country had put into motion.

That prompted Malta's prime minister, Joseph Muscat, to post a congratulatory tweet and proclaim the island's intention to be the "global trailblazers in the regulation of blockchain-based businesses."

But a month later, Binance's chief executive, Zhao Changpeng, traveled to Bermuda to announce that the company would also open up compliance operations there and invest $15 million in the island. At the signing event with Mr. Burt, Mr. Zhao wore a tie and blue Bermuda shorts.

Mr. Zhao did not respond to requests for comment.

Many of the countries passing the new laws have said they are not interested in becoming a home for illicit activity. Albert Isola, Gibraltar's finance minister, said his government was accustomed to making hard decisions after regulating online gambling companies for the last 25 years.

"For every one license we've issued, we've probably said no to 10," he said. "When you're considering a new sector, to bring in big names is extremely attractive, but they've got to be good names. So you've got to be willing to say no to even some of the bigger ones."

Online gambling is responsible for around 3,000 jobs on Gibraltar, or about 10 percent of the territory's population. Mr. Isola said he saw a similar possibility in the blockchain, calling it "the next significant new flow of business."

Gibraltar is in the final stages before voting on regulations that, similar to Malta's, would let companies issue and trade digital tokens. Already, 35 companies have applied to the government for licenses to operate blockchain businesses.

Liechtenstein, the Alpine nation between Austria and Switzerland, is also among the newer entrants to the race, with the prime minister circulating a Blockchain Act this summer to allow companies to sell tokens.

The activity has spread to other areas, too. Wyoming and Delaware have passed laws aimed at welcoming certain blockchain businesses, though they have been less focused on ones that trade in tokens. In 2014, New York created a so-called BitLicense, which initially drew businesses to the state, but it has since been viewed as a deterrent because of the government's wide-ranging requirements and slow approval process.

In Switzerland, the canton of Zug has also sought out crypto business, labeling itself Crypto Valley. Zug's top economic official who has worked on the effort, Guido Bulgheroni, flew to the cryptocurrency conference in May that Mr. Burt also attended.

At a cocktail party for Crypto Valley, Mr. Bulgheroni said his first job was to make sure that anyone with a crypto project was happy being in the Zug area.

"How many other jurisdictions have that?" he said.

Glossary

altcoin A cryptocurrency that is not Bitcoin.

Bitcoin The first cryptocurrency, developed by the pseudonymous Satoshi Nakamoto in 2008.

Bitcoin Cash A cryptocurrency that split from the original Bitcoin network to allow a higher number of coins to be created.

block Individual sections of a blockchain, permanently recording transactions and activities.

blockchain A decentralized public ledger that serves as the base of all cryptocurrency platforms.

cipherpunk A movement of computer programmers in the 1990s and 2000s who were interested in personal data security.

cryptocurrency A virtual currency created on a decentralized network of computers, maintained on a blockchain ledger.

decentralized application An application created for use on a blockchain like Ethereum.

Ethereum The second major cryptocurrency platform, developed by Vitalik Buterin in 2013.

fiat currency Currency issued by a government.

fork A split in a blockchain after disagreements over its administration, typically resulting in two competing cryptocurrencies.

halving The reduction of the amount of available coins that can be mined, designed in most cryptocurrencies to gradually limit the available supply.

HODL Misspelling of "hold," a term for keeping a cryptocurrency investment despite price volatility out of faith in the potential for cryptocurrency values to rise. It is also understood as an acronym meaning "hold on for dear life."

initial coin offering A means of fund-raising by selling a certain number of coins in advance of a new cryptocurrency release.

mining The process of generating new coins, involving the use of computing power to solve algorithmic puzzles.

peer to peer A type of decentralized computer network used in generating cryptocurrencies.

private key Encrypted password used to access private cryptocurrency.

proof of stake A consensus mechanism in adminstrating blockchains based in ownership of cryptocurrency, a less energy-intensive alternative to proof of work.

proof of work A consensus mechanism in administrating blockchains based on server contribution to the maintenance of the blockchain.

public key Encrypted password used to send cryptocurrency to another user.

Ripple A cryptocurrency platform developed in 2012 for use by banking institutions.

security A tradeable financial investment, including stocks, bonds and mutual funds. Many regulators advocate classifying cryptocurrencies as securities.

smart contract An automated contract between parties on a blockchain that rewards tasks with a defined amount of cryptocurrency.

token A coin-like component of an existing cryptocurrency platform specialized to a function of a decentralized application.

Media Literacy Terms

"Media literacy" refers to the ability to access, understand, critically assess and create media. The following terms are important components of media literacy, and they will help you critically engage with the articles in this title.

angle The aspect of a news story that a journalist focuses on and develops.

attribution The method by which a source is identified or by which facts and information are assigned to the person who provided them.

balance Principle of journalism that both perspectives of an argument should be presented in a fair way.

byline Name of the writer, usually placed between the headline and the story.

chronological order Method of writing a story presenting the details of the story in the order in which they occurred.

credibility The quality of being trustworthy and believable, said of a journalistic source.

editorial Article of opinion or interpretation.

feature story Article designed to entertain as well as to inform.

headline Type, usually 18 point or larger, used to introduce a story.

human interest story Type of story that focuses on individuals and how events or issues affect their life, generally offering a sense of relatability to the reader.

impartiality Principle of journalism that a story should not reflect a journalist's bias and should contain balance.

intention The motive or reason behind something, such as the publication of a news story.

interview story Type of story in which the facts are gathered primarily by interviewing another person or persons.

inverted pyramid Method of writing a story using facts in order of importance, beginning with a lead and then gradually adding paragraphs in order of relevance from most interesting to least interesting.

motive The reason behind something, such as the publication of a news story or a source's perspective on an issue.

news story An article or style of expository writing that reports news, generally in a straightforward fashion and without editorial comment.

op-ed An opinion piece that reflects a prominent individual's opinion on a topic of interest.

paraphrase The summary of an individual's words, with attribution, rather than a direct quotation of their exact words.

quotation The use of an individual's exact words indicated by the use of quotation marks and proper attribution.

reliability The quality of being dependable and accurate, said of a journalistic source.

rhetorical device Technique in writing intending to persuade the reader or communicate a message from a certain perspective.

tone A manner of expression in writing or speech.

Media Literacy Questions

1. The New York Times' first long piece on Bitcoin is an op-ed by Paul Krugman titled "Golden Cyberfetters" (on page 10). Why was this headline chosen, and how might it be used to communicate something about Bitcoin?

2. The author of "Why Bitcoin Matters" (on page 21) is Marc Andreessen, a businessperson with only a nominal amount of Bitcoin in his possession. Does ownership of Bitcoin introduce bias into an article?

3. Nathaniel Popper's "Decoding the Enigma of Satoshi Nakamoto and the Birth of Bitcoin" (on page 35) uses many sources to investigate the identity of Bitcoin's founder. What kinds of sources does he use, and which are most effective in reporting the story?

4. Mark T. Williams's "Bitcoin Is Not Yet Ready for the Real World" (on page 57) is an op-ed. Nick Wingfield's "Bitcoin Pursues the Mainstream" (on page 105) is a news story. How do the two stories differ in their treatment of the regulation of cryptocurrencies?

5. Identify the angle of Teddy Wayne's "Grandpa Had a Pension. This Generation Has Cryptocurrency." (on page 80). What aspect of millennial cryptocurrency investment does it focus on?

6. Kevin Roose's "Is There a Cryptocurrency Bubble? Just Ask Doge." (on page 87) focuses on the opinions of Dogecoin's creator. What is his motive for the points he makes about cryptocurrency bubbles?

7. Compare the headline of Nellie Bowles's "Everyone Is Getting Hilariously Rich and You're Not" (on page 93) with Noam Cohen's "Bubble or No, This Virtual Currency Is a Lot of Coin in Any Realm" (on page 69). How do these headlines differ in their approach to cryptocurrency bubbles?

8. Cao Li and Giulia Marchi's "In China's Hinterlands, Workers Mine Bitcoin for a Digital Fortune" (on page 123) is a human interest story, focusing on the workers at a Bitcoin mine. Who is the audience for this article?

9. Nathaniel Popper's article "Coinbase: The Heart of the Bitcoin Frenzy" (on page 128) includes quotations and paraphrased statements by Coinbase's CEO Brian Armstrong. What information is quoted, and what information is paraphrased?

10. Nathaniel Popper's article "Some Bitcoin Backers Are Defecting to Create a Rival Currency" (on page 167) uses an inverted pyramid structure. Compare the first paragraph with the last. Do you see a difference in importance in their subject matter?

11. Steven Johnson's "Beyond the Bitcoin Bubble" (on page 171) explores the long-term consequences of cryptocurrencies in depth. Does it display balance and impartiality?

12. Nellie Bowles's "Making a Crypto Utopia in Puerto Rico" (on page 197) is a human interest story. What audience might it be addressing? Compare it with the audience of "In China's Hinterlands, Workers Mine Bitcoin for a Digital Fortune" (on page 123).

Citations

All citations in this list are formatted according to the Modern Language Association's (MLA) style guide.

BOOK CITATION

NEW YORK TIMES EDITORIAL STAFF, THE. *Cryptocurrencies: Bitcoin, Blockchain and Beyond.* New York: New York Times Educational Publishing, 2019.

ONLINE ARTICLE CITATIONS

ANDREESSEN, MARC. "Why Bitcoin Matters." *The New York Times*, 21 Jan. 2014, https://dealbook.nytimes.com/2014/01/21/why-bitcoin-matters/.

BILTON, NICK. "Disruptions: A Digital Underworld Cloaked in Anonymity." *The New York Times*, 17 Nov. 2013, https://bits.blogs.nytimes.com/2013/11/17/disruptions-a-digital-underworld-cloaked-in-anonymity/.

BOWLES, NELLIE. "Everyone Is Getting Hilariously Rich and You're Not." *The New York Times*, 13 Jan. 2018, https://www.nytimes.com/2018/01/13/style/bitcoin-millionaires.html.

BOWLES, NELLIE. "Making a Crypto Utopia in Puerto Rico." *The New York Times*, 2 Feb. 2018, https://www.nytimes.com/2018/02/02/technology/cryptocurrency-puerto-rico.html.

CENTURY, ADAM. "Bitcoin Scandal Reflects Popularity of Virtual Currency in China." *The New York Times*, 17 Nov. 2013, https://sinosphere.blogs.nytimes.com/2013/11/17/bitcoin-scandal-reflects-popularity-of-virtual-currency-in-china/.

COHEN, NOAM. "Bubble or No, This Virtual Currency Is a Lot of Coin in Any Realm." *The New York Times*, 7 Apr. 2013, https://www.nytimes.com/2013/04/08/business/media/bubble-or-no-virtual-bitcoins-show-real-worth.html.

EMBER, SYDNEY. "Data Security Is Becoming the Sparkle in Bitcoin." *The New York Times*, 1 Mar. 2015, https://www.nytimes.com/2015/03/02/business/dealbook/data-security-is-becoming-the-sparkle-in-bitcoin.html.

FEUER, ALAN. "The Bitcoin Ideology." *The New York Times,* 14 Dec. 2013, https://www.nytimes.com/2013/12/15/sunday-review/the-bitcoin-ideology .html.

HARDY, QUENTIN. "Bitcoin Is a Protocol. Bitcoin Is a Brand." *The New York Times,* 6 Mar. 2014, https://bits.blogs.nytimes.com/2014/03/06/bitcoin-is-a -protocol-bitcoin-is-a-brand/.

HARDY, QUENTIN. "Ripple Aims to Put Every Transaction on One Ledger." *The New York Times,* 6 Apr. 2016, https://www.nytimes.com/2016/04/07/business /dealbook/ripple-aims-to-put-every-transaction-on-one-ledger.html.

JOHNSON, STEVEN. "Beyond the Bitcoin Bubble." *The New York Times,* 16 Jan. 2018, https://www.nytimes.com/2018/01/16/magazine/beyond-the-bitcoin -bubble.html.

KRUGMAN, PAUL. "Golden Cyberfetters." *The New York Times,* 7 Sept. 2011, https://krugman.blogs.nytimes.com/2011/09/07/golden-cyberfetters/.

LI, CAO, AND GIULIA MARCHI. "In China's Hinterlands, Workers Mine Bitcoin for a Digital Fortune." *The New York Times,* 13 Sept. 2017, https://www .nytimes.com/2017/09/13/business/bitcoin-mine-china.html.

MURPHY, KATE. "Virtual Currency Gains Ground in Actual World." *The New York Times,* 31 July 2013, https://www.nytimes.com/2013/08/01/technology /personaltech/virtual-currency-gains-ground-in-actual-world.html.

PERLROTH, NICOLE. "Anonymous Payment Schemes Thriving on Web." *The New York Times,* 29 May 2013, https://www.nytimes.com/2013/05/30 /technology/anonymous-payment-schemes-thriving-on-web.html.

PERLROTH, NICOLE. "To Instill Love of Bitcoin, Backers Work to Make It Safe." *The New York Times,* 1 Apr. 2014, https://dealbook.nytimes.com/2014 /04/01/to-instill-love-of-bitcoin-backers-work-to-make-it-safe/.

POPPER, NATHANIEL. "As Bitcoin Bubble Loses Air, Frauds and Flaws Rise to Surface." *The New York Times,* 5 Feb. 2018, https://www.nytimes.com /2018/02/05/tcchnology/virtual-currency-regulation.html.

POPPER, NATHANIEL. "Coinbase: The Heart of the Bitcoin Frenzy." *The New York Times,* 6 Dec. 2017, https://www.nytimes.com/2017/12/06/technology /coinbase-bitcoin.html.

POPPER, NATHANIEL. "Decoding the Enigma of Satoshi Nakamoto and the Birth of Bitcoin." *The New York Times,* 15 May 2015, https://www.nytimes .com/2015/05/17/business/decoding-the-enigma-of-satoshi-nakamoto-and -the-birth-of-bitcoin.html.

POPPER, NATHANIEL. "Easiest Path to Riches on the Web? An Initial Coin

Offering." *The New York Times*, 23 June 2017, https://www.nytimes.com
/2017/06/23/business/dealbook/coin-digital-currency.html.

POPPER, NATHANIEL. "Ethereum, a Virtual Currency, Enables Transactions
that Rival Bitcoin's." *The New York Times*, 27 Mar. 2016, https://www
.nytimes.com/2016/03/28/business/dealbook/ethereum-a-virtual-currency
-enables-transactions-that-rival-bitcoins.html.

POPPER, NATHANIEL. "Have a Cryptocurrency Company? Bermuda, Malta or
Gibraltar Wants You." *The New York Times*, 29 July 2018, https://www
.nytimes.com/2018/07/29/technology/cryptocurrency-bermuda-malta
-gibraltar.html.

POPPER, NATHANIEL. "How China Took Center Stage in Bitcoin's Civil War."
The New York Times, 29 June 2016, https://www.nytimes.com/2016/07/03
/business/dealbook/bitcoin-china.html.

POPPER, NATHANIEL. "How the Winklevoss Twins Found Vindication in a
Bitcoin Fortune." *The New York Times*, 19 Dec. 2017, https://www.nytimes
.com/2017/12/19/technology/bitcoin-winklevoss-twins.html.

POPPER, NATHANIEL. "In Bitcoin's Orbit: Rival Virtual Currencies Vie for
Acceptance." *The New York Times*, 24 Nov. 2013, https://dealbook.nytimes
.com/2013/11/24/in-bitcoins-orbit-rival-virtual-currencies-vie-for
-acceptance/.

POPPER, NATHANIEL. "Some Bitcoin Backers Are Defecting to Create a Rival
Currency." *The New York Times*, 25 July 2017, https://www.nytimes.com
/2017/07/25/business/dealbook/bitcoin-cash-split.html.

POPPER, NATHANIEL. "There Is Nothing Virtual About Bitcoin's Energy Appetite." *The New York Times*, 21 Jan. 2018, https://www.nytimes.com/2018
/01/21/technology/bitcoin-mining-energy-consumption.html.

POPPER, NATHANIEL. "A Venture Fund With Plenty of Capital, but No
Capitalist." *The New York Times*, 21 May 2016, https://www.nytimes
.com/2016/05/22/business/dealbook/crypto-ether-bitcoin-currency.html.

POPPER, NATHANIEL, AND NELLIE BOWLES. "Bitcoin Falls Below $10,000 as
Virtual Currency Bubble Deflates." *The New York Times*, 17 Jan. 2018,
https://www.nytimes.com/2018/01/17/technology/bitcoin-virtual-currency
-bubble.html.

POPPER, NATHANIEL, AND RACHEL ABRAMS. "Apparent Theft at Mt. Gox Shakes
Bitcoin World." *The New York Times*, 25 Feb. 2014, https://www.nytimes
.com/2014/02/25/business/apparent-theft-at-mt-gox-shakes-bitcoin
-world.html.

RAMZY, AUSTIN. "Chinese Bitcoin Investors Fret as Value of Virtual Currency Plunges." *The New York Times*, 19 Dec. 2013, https://sinosphere.blogs .nytimes.com/2013/12/19/chinese-bitcoin-investors-fret-as-value-of-virtual -currency-plunges/.

ROOSE, KEVIN. "Is There a Cryptocurrency Bubble? Just Ask Doge." *The New York Times*, 15 Sept. 2017, https://www.nytimes.com/2017/09/15/business /cryptocurrency-bubble-doge.html.

SOMMER, JEFF. "A Bitcoin Puzzle: Heads, It's Excitement. Tails, It's Anxiety." *The New York Times*, 23 Nov. 2013, https://www.nytimes.com/2013/11/24 /your-money/a-bitcoin-puzzle-heads-its-excitement-tails-its-anxiety.html.

WAYNE, TEDDY. "Grandpa Had a Pension. This Generation Has Cryptocurrency." *The New York Times*, 3 Aug. 2017, https://www.nytimes.com/2017 /08/03/style/what-is-cryptocurrency.html.

WILLIAMS, MARK T. "Bitcoin Is Not Yet Ready for the Real World." *The New York Times*, 24 Jan. 2014, https://dealbook.nytimes.com/2014/01/24/bitcoin -is-not-yet-ready-for-the-real-world/.

WINGFIELD, NICK. "Bitcoin Pursues the Mainstream." *The New York Times*, 30 Oct. 2013, https://www.nytimes.com/2013/10/31/technology/bitcoin -pursues-the-mainstream.html.

Index

This book is current up until the time of printing. For the most up-to-date reporting, visit www.nytimes.com.